Marketplace Leadership

Spiritual Tools for Today's Successful Leaders

Marketplace Leadership: Spiritual Tools for Today's Successful Leaders
Copyright ©2024 by Dale Jones

9 8 7 6 5 4 3 2 1

PRINTED IN THE UNITED STATES OF AMERICA
Heritage Publishing

ISBN: 9798218374501

Acknowledgments

We are the sum of those who believed in us, taught us, encouraged us, stood by us, and—yes, by some strange coincidence—doubted us along the way. I am eternally grateful for all my teachers, pastors, mentors, and coaches who inspired me to stay focused and to become better day by day.

I want to thank the many leaders, from Jack Welch (CEO, General Electric) to Harold Troy (my grade school coach), who saw something great in me even when I didn't see it myself. Their examples of leadership, by precept and example, have been life-changing and shaped my perspective as a leader.

I want to give a special thanks to Bishop Matthew L. Brown, who invited me to do a six-week Bible study on kingdom leadership in the marketplace at Greater Community Church in Marietta, Georgia. Those weeks of teaching were the catalyst and the inspiration I needed to fully step into this new season of my life, which culminated in the writing of this book.

Many thanks to my publisher, Johnny Stephens, and the entire Heritage Publishing family, who believed in me and this project from day one! Your enthusiasm kept me going even when the workdays became long and arduous.

And what can I say about the rock of our family, my wife, Kimberlyn Jones, who motivated, influenced, and advocated for me every step of the way? There were moments when I didn't think I had the patience to sit down and accomplish this task, but she was that driving force that constantly reminded me the world needed to hear from my years of experience.

I also acknowledge the many members of my former churches—Perfecting Faith and Kingdom Church—for their encouragement, love, and support. You gave me the experience that made me the kind of leader I am today.

Many thanks to my children, DJ and Whitney, for your patience and loving support when I spent countless hours serving others while occasionally missing some of the important moments in your lives. You are my pride and joy, and I will forever live to make you proud to call me "Dad."

Contents

Introduction

What is the significance of the marketplace, and what is our leadership responsibility in it? How should we understand the concept of work in the grand scheme of things? Is there a greater purpose to this common pursuit; or was King Solomon, the wisest man who ever lived, on the right track when he conjectured that the toils and anxieties of work are all meaningless? Solomon ultimately concluded that true fulfillment and joy of work can be achieved through enlightenment, which only comes from the wisdom and knowledge that God gives (Ecclesiastes 2:26, NIV).

It is this wisdom and knowledge that we seek to become more effective leaders in the marketplace and to accomplish those things that are God-inspired. The wisdom of this world is antithetical to God's wisdom, but most people have trafficked in it only to discover in the end that their labors, toils, and anxieties were all vanities and meaningless pursuits.

God has a plan and a purpose for every person on the planet. He has uniquely designed every one of us and has marked us such that the idea of competing with others is oxymoronic. Out of eight billion people on the planet, no one has your fingerprint, DNA, voiceprint, or pattern of the retina of your eye. You are uniquely created for this generation and this moment! Knowing God and understanding His creative plan for your life is essential to the work you are called to do on the planet.

Notwithstanding, knowledge is never enough, but applying what you know of God and His ultimate plan for creating you is practical wisdom. Throughout this book, we will discover that the concept of work was not an afterthought for God. Instead, it is central to His overall creative plan and subsequent to His redemptive plan to restore creative order to its original design.

Throughout my life, I knew God was preparing me differently. I never quite fit neatly into the conventional wisdom of the culture or society of my time. At 13, I had an indelible encounter with God that would shape my life forever. My father was a local pastor, and he instilled in his children a reverence for God. But at a young age, I didn't know the distinction between fear and reverence.

At 16, I was a youth leader and ministered at youth conferences in the Southeastern United States. While in high school, I was elected to various roles: sophomore class president, student representative, and vice president of the student council, which occasionally took me away from church.

At the end of my junior year, I was the only candidate for president of the student council. However, I was advised by church leadership to focus my attention and energy on pursuing church matters rather than activities at school. I was confused by that; however, I complied and removed my name from the ballot for student council president. I later wondered how effective I could have been as a believer and as president.

After graduating high school, I enrolled in North Carolina State University, where I studied electrical engineering and graduated with honors in 1987 and started work at General Electric. During my first year, I received a patent for my work in protecting fiber optics communication from outside intruders. My engineering work led me to the GE management program, where I quickly excelled.

My journey led me to global assignments as general manager and senior executive of worldwide sourcing with a budget of $3.6 billion and a staff on every major continent. Another assignment gave me broader responsibility as president and CEO of GE Clinical Service, Inc., a subsidiary company of GE Medical System.

While my career flourished, I also excelled at church, where I took on several leadership roles, including assistant pastor. By now, I was struggling again with what I perceived to be the daily transition between the secular space, which I call "the marketplace," and the sacred space called "the church." I was constantly beset with whether God was displeased with my "lack of total commitment" to the work of the church, which was instilled in me as a child. After 18 years of working in the corporate world, I felt the call to do something different, so I retired in 2005.

In September 2001, my wife, Kimberlyn, and I, along with our two children, launched Perfecting Faith Ministry as a local church in Nashville, Tennessee. During this time, I began a deep study into the kingdom of God, which led to a greater understanding of God's original intention for work and His call to kingdom dominion in the earth. This shifted my message significantly as a pastor to this newly gathered congregation.

The ministry attracted prominent business leaders and entrepreneurs and quickly became one of the fastest-growing churches in the community. The ministry focused on the marketplace and leadership as we instructed believers, based on the Great Commission, to go into every space, arena, crevice, and corner of the world and change, influence, and impact it for Christ.

If we are to be the light of the world, it's important to understand that light is best seen in dark places. God does not want us to run from darkness but rather to run to it. Jesus told his disciples that He was sending them out as sheep among wolves. There is no time for the church to retreat into obscurity but to advance and take the kingdom of God by force.

During the same time of our pastorate, Kimberlyn began a cosmetology school with her hairstylist to take that industry to the next level. In the space of seven years, we grew the school from one location to five in three states while revenue grew from $120,000 to over $12,000,000.

As the business and church expanded, we ministered effectively in both arenas. Students and staff members were transformed by the gospel while workers, lay people, and leaders grew and became more impactful in the marketplace. For the first time, I felt no contradictions or apprehensions between the sacred space of the church and the secular environment of the marketplace. Both existed for a grander purpose of giving glory to God.

As pastors, we gave instructions in the sacred space on becoming effective witnesses and change agents in the secular space and watched people seamlessly navigate both. We discovered that one was no good without the other.

After 18 years as a local pastor, I felt the call again to do something different. I did not understand what God was doing in my life; however, He had molded me in such a unique way to have experienced the corporate space at a high level for 18 years, the church world at a pastoral level for 18 years, and the entrepreneurial world at a substantial level. Those experiences informed me what God wanted to do next in my life.

The number *18* represents bondage, oppression, and limitation. However, from a spiritual perspective, it represents spiritual awakening, finding purpose, and the power of infinite possibilities. When the number is repeated twice, it signifies liberation and freedom. The angel number *1818* encourages us to break free from all forms of limitations and embrace the freedom to pursue our true potential.

In 2023, Kimberlyn and I joined Greater Community Church in Marietta, Georgia, under the leadership of Bishop Matthew L. Brown, who is one of the most consequential leaders of our time. His desire to grow and develop his congregation members' lives in every area is unmatched.

After several months, Pastor Brown asked us to teach a four-week Sunday school class on the kingdom of God in the marketplace. Four weeks led to six weeks of powerful teaching on God's original intention for those who bear his image to take dominion in the marketplace. This is God's original mandate for His people and what He is calling for us to live out today. Those weeks of teaching on the marketplace solidified what God called us to do in the next phase of our lives: to develop the next generation of marketplace leaders for the kingdom of God.

What is so important about the marketplace? The church, as we know it today, is losing its relevance. Less than 20 percent of the population in the United States attends church regularly. By 2050, church attendance is projected to drop to 11.7 percent. On the other hand, 85 percent of Christians' waking hours are spent in the marketplace, and almost all non-Christians are in the marketplace.[1]

Indeed, there is an army of born-again believers that is currently traversing through the marketplace who need to be awakened to their God-ordained dominion in the earth. Like me, some are apprehensive and sometimes timid in their approach to the marketplace. Others are having to dumb down their creative and innovative instinct to fit into a culture that is often intimidated by them. They need to be empowered with the wisdom and knowledge that only comes from God to make the qualitative difference in the world they are called to occupy.

God desires more from His people. Retreating to church on Sunday and timidly showing up to the marketplace on Monday is not God's idea of dominion. Speaking in tongues and prophesying to one another is not God's idea of dominion. Changing the environment around us through creative and innovative means while boldly confessing the name of Christ is the stuff of kingdom dominion. The marketplace is the final frontier for the church that we must not concede. God has set apostles, evangelists, pastors, prophets, and teachers in the church to perfect and equip it to powerfully navigate the marketplace, which is everything outside the church.

As the church inches closer to the millennial reign of Christ, better known as "the age of the kingdom," we are called to represent a powerful and creative God in powerful and creative ways. As such, we need committed pastors, specialized teachers, and emboldened evangelists and prophets who have dedicated themselves to equip the church to become "more able." Marketplace ministries can never take the place of these God-given gifts to the body of Christ, but the ministry must become the vehicle by which we convince men to become followers of Christ.

As the *ekklesia* ("the church"; "the called-out ones"), we are the salt of the earth and the light of the world! The marketplace cannot "see" or function without us. It is God who ordained work and called us all to it. Work should not be seen as drudgery but as a noble and dignified pursuit. It was God who created us and gave us the assignment of work; therefore, work should become our reasonable service to God. We must take our rightful place in the marketplace and provide the leadership needed to bring the world one step closer to God.

Unfortunately, we tend to pursue the wrong things that have no eternal or intrinsic value to the kingdom of God. These pursuits will always leave us anxious about our future with a desire for self-preservation rather than self-actualization. Our coworkers and bosses ought to see God in us, not just in what we say, but in what we do and accomplish. Every place of employment should be seeking the wisdom, insight, and skills of born-again believers, but sadly, some of us don't see our worth and relevance in the marketplace.

We should know that in everything God has called us to do, He has already given provision for it. There is no lack or scarcity in God. We are uniquely created, called, and qualified to accomplish the purpose to which God has called us on the planet. Before we got here, God had already equipped us with everything we needed to win. Wealth and prosperity are already on the path God has ordained for us to take.

Our job is never to give in to anxiety but to actualize what God has purposed for us to do in our generation without fear or intimidation. The world is waiting for us to show up in our authentic selves. Indeed, the earth groans in earnest expectation for the revelation of the sons of God.

As born-again believers, we are the sons of God that all creation is earnestly waiting to see. We are called, and we have a duty to show up to allow God to carry out His purpose and to do superabundantly more than all that we dare ask or think, infinitely beyond our greatest prayers, hopes, or dreams, according to His power that is at work within us (Ephesians 3:20, AMP).

[1]"7 Reasons Why the Marketplace Is a Great Place for Christians," by Darren Shearer, Theology of Business Institute.

Chapter One

Christ in the Marketplace

The modern church often finds itself preoccupied with the same territory and surroundings: the church building. However, our call to worship and serve God extends beyond the walls of the church. Our worship is not confined to the sanctuary but must thrive in the marketplace—the vast, diverse world where daily life unfolds.

This is a vital arena for ministry, and the time to act is now. In embracing the marketplace as a crucial aspect of our mission, we align ourselves with God's broader plan for His creation. By stepping out of our comfort zones and into the dynamic environments of the marketplace, we answer the call to make disciples of all nations.

The marketplace offers limitless opportunities for ministry, and our involvement in these spaces is crucial to advancing the kingdom of God. Our work and worship should extend into every aspect of our lives. Whether in our workplaces, schools, neighborhoods, or online communities, we are called to be a transformative presence, demonstrating God's love and truth in tangible ways.

Anatomy of the Marketplace

Week after week, millions of Christians sit in sanctuaries where we worship, listen to sermons, participate in various ministries, and fellowship with one another. While we may feel quite satisfied and virtuous with our faithful attendance each week, much more is required to live purpose-filled, impactful lives. We weren't born again and called to the kingdom of God to go to church. While church attendance is vital to the enabling and strengthening of every born-again believer, the purpose to which we are called is to be the conduit through which God reconciles the world to Himself. Church attendance is merely the huddle from which we break to do the work of changing the world for Christ.

Each one of us was born, shaped, and purposed in our generation to make maximum impact on the world in which we live and to change the environment in which we find ourselves. We are called to be salt, light, and yeast in a world that is increasingly dominated by cultural preferences and norms. In other words, we are called to be thermostats and not merely thermometers to change the atmosphere wherever we go. Jesus was moved with compassion as He looked over His surroundings because He understood His purpose and said to His disciples, "The harvest is [indeed] plentiful, but the workers are few."[a]

Where do I start? we wonder. Many of us may resort to well-worn outreach methods. We invite family members to go to church with us, we go with a group to knock on doors and pass out leaflets, or we visit homeless missions to talk about the gospel with those less fortunate. While these methods have value, these go-to approaches are well within our comfort zone, and they limit our reach. But what if I told you God is calling us to something much bigger?

Welcome to the marketplace!

Marketplace (Greek: *agora*) is defined as "gathering place." While that definition does indeed include our church sanctuaries, the marketplace is vastly larger than all the sanctuaries in the world combined. That's because the marketplace is any gathering place anywhere! If that's too broad of a definition, let's dissect it. Let's look at the anatomy of the marketplace where God has called us to minister.

Many Christians dismiss anything outside the sanctuary as being "of the world"; thus, some of us have missed God's call to go out into that same world and spread the gospel to everyone. Before His ascension, Jesus told His disciples, "You will be My witnesses [to tell people about Me] both in Jerusalem and in all Judea, and Samaria, and even to the ends of the earth."[b]

If we look more carefully at what Jesus was saying, we'll see that He first named Jerusalem, where the disciples already were (in other words, "their home turf"). They lived, worked, and knew many people in and around the Holy City, so they would probably feel extremely comfortable spreading the gospel there.

However, Jesus expanded their circle to include Judea, the region surrounding Jerusalem, and Samaria, an area several days journey from Jerusalem. When He said they should go "even to the ends of the earth," that was a clear sign that they would need to leave their home synagogues and familiar surroundings to fulfill Jesus' commands.

God's mission was much larger than the places they already knew. So to obey God's commission, they would need to go into the marketplace, which would include gathering places far beyond where they felt comfortable.

Where is your marketplace? Whether you know it or not, you're probably in your marketplace right now. For example, when you show up at your company, the school you or your children attend, your neighborhood, your social media accounts, community centers, banks, hospitals, the beach, city hall, playgrounds, restaurants, airports, prisons, hotels, and movie theaters, you are in the marketplace. Put simply, the marketplace is where people gather and is found anywhere outside the church walls.

We need to explore the limitless possibilities of the marketplace because I want to encourage believers to go beyond the brick-and-mortar church so they can minister to the "whole person." When we refuse to share our faith beyond our church silos, we tend to address only the spiritual needs of those people who come to our churches or those persons in our go-to places where we feel somewhat comfortable talking about Christ.

But human beings are spirit, mind, and body, and we neglect a major portion of what God has called us to do when we stay exclusively within our church buildings. We can't be effective leaders if we try to appeal only to people's spirits while ignoring everything else about them and avoiding people who may never come to our churches.

Of course, the spiritual part of our lives is critically important, but we spend about 92 percent of our time in the marketplace as compared to the time we spend at church, so we must be prepared to spread the gospel wherever other people gather, wherever that may be. God is telling the church to occupy all those spaces they frequent every day and be light in those dark places. I'm amplifying that call to the church: Don't get so comfortable in the pews, but be a light for Christ in all the gathering places outside the church walls. Show up in the marketplace!

Why the Marketplace?

When we understand that the marketplace is everywhere outside the church, it's easier for us to unpack the "why" of the marketplace. God calls us to venture outside the church and find those places where the sacred meets the secular, where we can bring light and truth to those who live in darkness.

In the first portion of The Great Commission,[c] Jesus tells His disciples, "*Go* therefore and make disciples of *all the nations*" (emphasis added). For us to "make disciples of all the nations," first we must "go"! Indeed, Christ mandates us to go, not come. But many believers want to retreat to the church, where we end up preaching to one another week after week, rather than going out into the world to occupy the marketplace. We tell ourselves that we're in the world but not of it, which is our way of avoiding engagement with people we hold at arms' length, but the people who need to hear the gospel are waiting for us out there.

We must show unbelievers what being people of faith is all about. Many unbelievers have not only heard unflattering things about us, but they've had negative experiences with those who claim the name of Jesus. In some places, Christianity has earned a bad reputation, and people are wary of us. We must change that, but we can't do it from the pews. We must go out into the world and live out the gospel where we have a better chance to display the fruit of the Spirit.[d]

As leaders, we must embrace all the environs of the marketplace and not limit ourselves to areas where we find those persons who think just like we do. The reality is that we will encounter people who don't share our ideologies, habits, thoughts, vision, or ideas, but embracing this kind of cognitive diversity is critical to engaging with diverse people who are in our surroundings.

A company recently asked me to teach a seminar on the power of cultural diversity, but upon careful deliberation, I asked the conference host to allow me to elevate the conversation to engage the participants on cognitive diversity instead. While cultural diversity is a necessary topic in the marketplace, it is merely skin-deep. However, when we understand diversity at the thought level, encouraging people to think independently and critically, we can appreciate and benefit from the distinct giftings, talents, and ideas God has given to those we encounter.

This is the same approach I take in the church. I want to go beyond denominations and be comfortable in any space. When I teach the Word of God, I teach in such a way as to help people of faith question "the way we've always done things." I'm not necessarily trying to destroy the landmarks and traditions of the church because those have led us through the roughest of seasons.

Instead, I want to shake people out of their comfort zones and encourage them to get out and explore the marketplace with fresh eyes. The company you work for is more than where you go to clock in and out so you can get a check two weeks later. You can do more at the grocery store than buy food, and you may find that you can do more at the gym than just work out.

I also want to dispel the myth that Christ hung out in the temple. Jesus' lineage was not that of the Levites, so He didn't descend from the priestly tribe and wouldn't qualify to be a temple leader. Even when He taught in the synagogue, the people were astonished and then offended by Him: "Many who listened to Him were astonished, saying, 'Where did this man get these things [this knowledge and spiritual insight]? What is this wisdom [this confident understanding of the Scripture] that has been given to Him, and such miracles as these performed by His hands? Is this not the carpenter. . . ?' And they were [deeply] offended by Him [and their disapproval blinded them to the fact that He was anointed by God as the Messiah]."[e] The people in the synagogue identified Jesus as a marketplace leader, not as a priest.

Scripture confirms that Jesus spent most of His time in the marketplace. He went to "villages, or cities, or the countryside"[f] where "they were laying the sick in the market places."[g] This verse shows us that friends and family members of those who were sick sought help in the marketplaces and not the synagogues. That might irritate those of us who are used to people lining up at the altar to be healed.

I'm not saying there's no place for that because those of us who are part of the body of Christ need healing, too, and this can happen in our sanctuaries. However, many people may never enter our temples, assemblies, worship centers, or cathedrals, but they still hunger for healing and wholeness. How will they receive God's healing power if we don't go out into the marketplace to be God's hands and feet?

I'm not telling anyone to stop going to church, but sometimes our sanctuaries can become sterile and sanitized, untouched by the ills of the human condition. We might find the marketplace scary and dangerous, and Jesus knew we might have such encounters. He told His disciples, "Behold, I send you forth as sheep in the midst of wolves: be ye therefore wise as serpents, and harmless as doves."[h] But Jesus promises to be with us: "I am with you always, even unto the end of the world."[i]

Jesus went where there were needs, even if the conditions and the people were unsavory. He hung out in places where people were living, working, playing, loving, and dying. This way, He saw people struggle with adversity, sin, and death. And just as Jesus hung out in the places where life was happening all around Him, so should we: "In this [union and fellowship with Him], love is completed *and* perfected with us, so that we may have confidence in the day of judgment [with assurance and boldness to face Him]; *because as He is, so are we in this world"*[j] (emphasis added). When people find Christ in the market-place, they should find us, too. We are the body of Christ, so what are our hands doing? Where are our feet going? What are our eyes seeing? We are His representatives, so we must go where He would go and do what He would do.

If we want to make an impact in the marketplace, we could use the following practical applications:

Identify our marketplaces. Believers have unique mar-ketplaces based on their daily interactions and spheres of influence. These could be corporate offices, classrooms, neigh-borhoods, and online platforms. Recognizing these spaces as mission fields is the first step toward effective marketplace ministry.

Engage with purpose. To engage the marketplace mean-ingfully, believers must approach it with intentionality and purpose. This involves being attentive to the needs and oppor-tunities within these spaces, building genuine relationships, and demonstrating the love of Christ through words and actions. It also requires a willingness to step out of comfort zones and engage with diverse perspectives and backgrounds.

Overcome challenges. Marketplace ministry is not with-out its challenges. Believers may encounter resistance, skepti-cism, or hostility. However, these challenges can be met with wisdom, humility, and resilience. Jesus' instruction to be "wise as serpents and innocent as doves"[k] provides a guiding prin-ciple for navigating complex and often hostile environments.

Embrace innovation. As society evolves, so too must the methods of marketplace ministry. Embracing technology and innovative approaches can enhance the reach and impact of ministry efforts. This includes leveraging social media, digital platforms, and creative initiatives to connect with people in new and dynamic ways.

Develop a marketplace mindset. To have a marketplace mindset, continuous learning and adaptation are essential. Believers must remain attuned to cultural shifts, emerging needs, and opportunities for engagement. This involves ongoing training, discipleship, and support from church leadership to equip and empower people for effective marketplace ministry.

Being a marketplace minister involves using one's business as a platform for kingdom work. It's about seeing business as a vocation through which one can fulfill God's mandate to steward and cultivate the earth.

Live out ethical business practices. Conducting business with integrity and fairness reflects God's character. Living in this way builds trust with customers and employees and sets a standard for others in the industry.

Invest in employee care. Treating employees well, providing fair wages, and creating a positive work environment align with biblical principles of justice and love. When we care for employees, we recognize the inherent value of each person made in the image of God.

Provide community support. Using business profits to support local communities and charitable causes demonstrates the love of Christ. A business that is present and active in the lives of those who live and work in that community indicates that the business is not solely focused on profit but also on making a positive impact.

Establish sustainable practices. Implementing sustainable and environmentally friendly practices reflects the biblical mandate to care for creation. It acknowledges that we are stewards of the earth and responsible for its well-being.

Investing time in the marketplace may seem antithetical to what we have traditionally done as believers, but God calls us to co-create with Him, and we need to be relentless. As we undertake this important work, we need to be busy and engaged until He returns.

Jesus taught a parable about a nobleman preparing to do business in a far-off country. Before he left, he called his servants together, gave them ten pounds, and said, "Occupy till I come."[1] The man expected his servants to be busy while he was away, not idle. This parable is similar to the more familiar parable of the talents,[m] which comes after the parable of the ten virgins.[n] In each of these parables, there is an expectation of preparation and busyness while they are waiting.

From the beginning, God worked and expects us to work. "There was not a man to till the ground."[o] The word *till* means to "work, to serve, and worship," so Adam and Eve's work was their worship. That's what the kingdom of God is all about, and our services can be rendered anywhere outside the temple. There was no temple or any other house of worship in the garden of Eden. So where did Adam and Eve work and serve? Right where they were: the garden. This takes us back to God's original intention, which is for us to work, serve, and worship where we are. There is a plan and purpose for the church, but we don't have to wait until we get there to be busy doing God's work.

When my wife and I were thinking about entering the cosmetology industry, I was uncertain if this was the path for us. We were comfortable building the new church location God had called us to lead and didn't want to enter the "darkness" of the marketplace, but the Lord immediately convicted us. He reminded us that we represent light, and what better place for light to be seen than in dark places? That's all I needed to hear. I knew then that God was also calling us to new territories in the marketplace where we could be leaders and spread light.

Once we made those first steps into the industry, we met people hungry for God but had been negatively affected by people in the church. They had experiences that drove them away from God. But God brought us into that space, and we ministered to them. We found that their perception of God had been distorted by negative experiences, which made them believe they had no place in God's kingdom or among God's people. If we had waited until the people we met decided to come to our church, we would still be waiting.

A 2022 survey shows that 31 percent of Americans never attend church.[1] That's 31 percent of people who won't come to us, so we must go to them. We heeded God's commission to go, and we were able to share the love of God. We didn't try to change their behavior. We left that in God's hands, but our assignment was to introduce God and show them His love.

Many of us memorized John 3:16 as children, and we've quoted the verse so many times that it may not have the impact on us that it once had. But how powerful those words are! If you're asking, "Why the marketplace?" John 3:16 succinctly gives us our "why." "For God so loved *the world*" (emphasis added) confirms that God's love goes beyond our church walls.

We can't remain sequestered inside our church buildings. There's a world full of people out there in the marketplace who need us to show up where they can see us and our light. They need to meet the God who loves them and cares about them. But to introduce them to our great God, we must leave our comfort zones and move with urgency to the places God calls us to go.

The call to engage with the marketplace is a profound reminder of our broader mission as followers of Christ. The marketplace, representing all places where people gather outside the traditional church setting, is a vast and dynamic field ripe for the harvest. This concept challenges us to move beyond the comfort and confines of our church sanctuaries and step into the world where everyday life happens.

Jesus' ministry serves as a model for us; He did not limit His interactions to the synagogue but spent significant time in the marketplace, meeting people where they were. Similarly, we are called to the world to bring light into dark places and to be active witnesses in every corner of the world, with people in diverse community, and with diverse world views.

Ultimately, our engagement with the marketplace is about embodying the gospel in all its fullness, showing up where people are, and being a beacon of hope and healing in a broken world. As we heed this call, we fulfill our purpose as the body of Christ, actively participating in God's redemptive work and bringing His light to every corner of creation.

Chapter Two

The Intersection of Work and Faith

Ministry in the marketplace is essential, integrating faith with everyday life. Marketplace ministry draws on Jesus' teachings to illustrate how believers can fulfill their calling in various spheres of society. Our journey toward kingdom leadership encounters the value of work and its strategic placement within God's plan. Our professions, relationships, and daily encounters can become platforms for demonstrating the love and truth of Christ.

We honor those called to minister within the church and emphasize the critical role of those called to the marketplace. It is a divine mandate to ensure the gospel penetrates every corner of society. We can effectively disciple others in the marketplace, balancing work and witness, but we can't be complacent or inconsistent. By integrating our faith with our work and daily lives, we can create opportunities for meaningful conversations and relationships that draw others to Christ. This approach requires wisdom, discernment, and a commitment to excellence in our work, reflecting the values of the kingdom of God.

We can harness the power of the marketplace for God's glory. By embracing our unique callings and working together as a diverse body of believers, we can extend our reach and impact the world around us. Through the guidance of the Holy Spirit, we must learn to navigate the challenges and opportunities of the marketplace, making disciples and building God's kingdom everywhere on earth.

The marketplace is not just a backdrop; it is the frontline where believers are called to fulfill their divine mission. This is not a leisurely journey but a pressing march toward kingdom leadership, recognizing the profound value of work and its strategic place in God's grand design. Every interaction, every relationship, and every professional encounter must become a powerful platform to demonstrate the love and truth of Christ.

Jesus Showed Up Where He Was Needed

Why do we find Jesus in the marketplace? His presence there was significant because He saw the experiences of everyday people and had compassion for them. His mission was to show up where people needed Him. "When He saw the crowds, He was moved with compassion *and* pity for them, because they were dispirited and distressed, like sheep without a shepherd."[a]

Jesus understood His assignment and what He was there to do. But because He worked among the people and not in an ivory tower far removed from them, Jesus could meet them where they were. "We have not an high priest which cannot be touched with the feeling of our infirmities; but was in all points tempted like as we are, yet without sin."[b]

Can we be touched by those we meet at the gas station, at our child's daycare, at work, at the airport, or on social media? People all around us are distressed, dejected, discouraged, and adrift. Are we accessible? Can we feel compassion toward those who don't think like we do, those who don't share our ideological biases, or those who sit beside us in our sanctuaries?

As leaders, we must discover ways to navigate the marketplace and harness that power while remaining available and relevant. We must learn how to shepherd the army of believers who spend 92 percent of their time outside the church and empower them to extend their reach to those around them.

The Gospels confirm that Jesus' presence outside the temple and the synagogue made Him much more accessible. He made 92 percent of His public appearances in the marketplace. Of all the parables He told, 87 percent have references to the marketplace, and 86 percent of His miracles took place there. Jesus gives us a master class on how to work the marketplace, where He was the most effective, and not remain in the confines of the synagogue, where many people found Him offensive. His example models for us what the kingdom of God looks like.

Balancing Temple and Marketplace Leadership

While God calls most of us to minister in the marketplace, He also calls a group of people to minister to the body of Christ. Like the Levitical priests before them, this group is assigned essential roles in the temple where they prepare the rest of us to spread the gospel to the masses.

Today, we refer to these assignments as "the five-fold ministry." The apostle Paul wrote, "And he gave some, apostles; and some, prophets; and some, evangelists; and some, pastors and teachers; For the perfecting of the saints, for the work of the ministry, for the edifying of the body of Christ."[c] The word *edify* means "to make more useful," so these ecclesiastical giftings help make the people of God more useful in the marketplace.

As we explore this concept of kingdom leadership, we will discuss the value of work and how it strategically positions us in the marketplace. But we can never forget or dismiss the value of the work of those persons whose ministry is to the church. I will always encourage God's people to take their witness as far outside their comfort zones as possible, wherever people gather, but I also want to emphasize the importance of those who prepare and equip us to serve and do effective work in the marketplace.

Those called to the temple are an essential part of God's plan to reach far beyond the church, even to the "uttermost part of the earth."[d] We can't go into the marketplace without them. We need their edification, encouragement, exhortation, admonition, and guidance. Our modern-day priests must be free to exercise their giftings and not be forced to be bi-vocational or take on the stress of establishing careers outside the church. Just as we focus mainly on marketplace leadership, those persons called to the work of the church are called to temple leadership.

We appreciate those teachers and professors who taught us, yet they remained in academia after we left school to enter the workforce. We also value those pastors, teachers, preachers, evangelists, apostles, and prophets who prepare us to enter the marketplace as they remain devoted to the work of the church. This balance creates the perfect environment for God's kingdom to be built and His will to be done in the earth. Thank God for those who are called full-time to minister to the body of Christ!

Making Disciples in the Marketplace

When gathering His disciples, Jesus chose men from diverse backgrounds and professions. He looked for cognitive diversity rather than exclusively cultural diversity. Jesus followed in the footsteps of His earthly father, Joseph, and became a carpenter. But we don't find in Scripture where there was another carpenter among His chosen disciples.

Instead, Jesus chose men of varying socioeconomic classes, ideologies, and occupations. Peter, James, and John were working-class fishermen, which was quite different from the middle-class or upper-middle-class professions of Simon, a politician, and Judas, an accountant. Matthew was in a class of his own since he was a tax collector, a despised profession.

Jesus understood all the different giftings that His disciples provided, and it was His job to cultivate and develop those giftings to turn the world upside down. Kingdom leaders today must also recognize the value of diverse gifts and experiences among those they serve. The marketplace provides countless opportunities to disciple people from various walks of life. Effective discipleship requires discernment and adaptability, tailored to the specific context and persons involved. The marketplace offers us many opportunities to disciple people for Christ.

It's not a question of *if* we can make disciples in the marketplace; it's *how* we disciple the people around us. Leaders must develop the discernment necessary to know how to make disciples the right way. When I consider discipling in the marketplace, I don't have a one-size-fits-all approach. How I participate in discipleship will depend on where I am, the people I want to reach, and other variables I must consider. Some of us preach when we should be working, or we stay silent when we should speak up.

For example, as a CEO, I don't want those who work for me to spend eight hours on the clock preaching to their coworkers. I pay them to work those hours, but if they spend it preaching, they likely won't achieve the results for which they were hired. Thus, I'm paying for work they didn't do. I expect employees to come to work and do their jobs because that work will speak louder than any sermon they might preach. At the same time, I want believers to show their light so people see a difference in them. It's not just what they do but how they do what they do that makes a difference. I would be disappointed if they were frequently late for work, spent more time complaining, or were reprimanded for ethics violations.

When I worked at GE, my work got results. I was promoted, and my coworkers noticed my work ethic and success and were drawn to that. They would ask, "How did you do that?" "You're only 36. How are you so successful?" My success opened the door for conversation, and when they would ask questions, I would ask them, "Do you want to know the truth, or do you want the politically correct answer?" When they said they wanted to know the truth, I would tell them to see me after work. That's when I could talk freely about my walk with God and His enabling power working through me to do more than I thought possible.

I didn't start that discussion during the workday because my assignment was to honor God with my work, not cheat the company by not working. So I didn't linger in the breakroom or hang around the water cooler preaching to coworkers when I should have been working. Neither did I join in with other people who were complaining about the work environment. Instead, my work ethic, consistency, and success caused people to want to know more.

When our work is exemplary, it is seen as a light in dark places. This is one way that God's glory is seen through our work. We become the embodiment of the life of Christ, and people will want to know what's so different about us and how they can live similar lives. We show Christ fully formed in us, and we live that out every day. By following Jesus' example, we can make disciples in the marketplace.

Jesus understood His disciples more than anyone else. He understood their passions and failures, their strengths and weaknesses, their propensities and their proclivities, yet He called them to participate with Him to change the world. He saw what was in them, He knew their worth and what they had to offer God's kingdom: gifts that would not be fully realized until after He ascended. He also understood how to bring out the best in them.

We may find Peter's personality a bit grating, but Jesus knew exactly who Peter was, including his quirks, flaws, strengths, and weaknesses. He knew Peter had a fiery personality and that he was impulsive, that he was quick to speak but didn't necessarily think things through.

Jesus needed a maverick and a firebrand like Peter to be bold and courageous. Guess who stood up on the Day of Pentecost and delivered a brilliant sermon? Peter. Of course, by then, he was more mature and disciplined, but he could speak to the multitudes about the power of the Holy Spirit.

John wrote the Gospel of John and the Johannine epistles (1, 2, 3 John). He laid his head on Jesus' shoulder at the Last Supper. Jesus needed John's love and compassion to encourage believers to love God and one another. Simon was a zealot. He was part of a group that today we might compare to jihadis. Jesus needed a passionate statesman who would resist Roman occupation.

Matthew was thought of as not much better than a crook and a grifter. As a tax collector, it was his job to collect money from his fellow Jews to give to the Roman authorities, and it was assumed that he would also skim a bit off the top for himself. But Jesus needed someone despised by his own people to be on His team.

Even Judas, "the son of perdition," had a purpose. He betrayed Jesus, but that didn't come as a surprise. So before we self-righteously condemn Judas, we must remember that he was pivotal to God's plan. Jesus needed a traitor to set in motion the events that led to his finished work on the cross and, ultimately, our means of salvation.

From the marketplace, Jesus assembled this ragtag, disparate group of men. They were remarkably different from one another and had their flaws and issues. But as a team, they radically impacted the world for generations. Jesus knows us better than we know ourselves, but He can still use us to change the world and do great things. He will show us how to carry ourselves in the marketplace, how to fulfill our assignment outside the church, and how to make kingdom disciples with people who are vastly different from us.

In His Sermon on the Mount, Jesus taught that we should make an impact by becoming salt and light wherever we go:

> Ye are the salt of the earth: but if the salt has lost his savor, wherewith shall it be salted? it is thenceforth good for nothing, but to be cast out, and to be trodden under foot of men. Ye are the light of the world. A city that is set on a hill cannot be hid. Neither do men light a candle, and put it under a bushel, but on a candlestick; and it giveth light unto all that are in the house. Let your light so shine before men, that they may see your good works, and glorify your Father which is in heaven.[f]

In this passage from the Sermon on the Mount, Jesus is giving us a master class on how we should show up in the marketplace. Just as salt adds flavor and light dispels darkness, through the power of the Holy Spirit, we should make a difference no matter where we are. That's why our presence is so necessary in all areas of society. Most of us traverse the marketplace every day, and it may seem that we're not making much of an impact out there, but that's not true.

When we view our interactions in the marketplace through the lens of faith, we can see many opportunities to bear witness to the love and light of Christ. We shouldn't give up on making disciples in the everyday spaces we find ourselves in.

Writer Darren Shearer gives seven reasons why the presence of Christians in the marketplace is a great idea and part of our divine call.[1]

Most non-Christians are in the marketplace. A growing number of people in the United States and Europe don't attend church regularly, so how do we reach them? We do that by meeting people where they are: at work, at the grocery store, on vacation, at school, in our neighborhood, and in any of the places we go outside church.

Most Christians are in the marketplace. We spend much of our time in the marketplace, and that makes it the perfect place for us to reach people. Shearer writes, "The marketplace is the primary context in which our spiritual gifts should be used. The ministry potential for Christians using their spiritual gifts collaboratively in the marketplace is astounding!"

Discipleship actually can happen in the marketplace. We may be more focused on getting people to go to church with us, but most of the discipleship process begins in the marketplace. Given how much time we spend with co-workers, clients, family members, and neighbors in various places, that equals more time than the few hours we spend each week at church.

The marketplace is a more authentic showroom of Christianity. Unbelievers get to see us in ways they would probably never see us at church. They see us engage with people, they see how we handle stress, and they see in real-time how we live out our Christianity in real-world situations. How we show up in the marketplace might influence whether the people we meet there want what we have.

The marketplace forces the church to use all its capabilities. The marketplace is so vast and there are so many needs to be met that every single Christian using every single spiritual gift is needed. "We need to approach marketplace ministry in a way that leverages the spiritual gifts of all Christians in the marketplace. The 'one-size-fits-all' approach only produces self-condemnation and ineffectiveness for marketplace Christians attempting to operate outside of their God-given spiritual gifts."

Denominational divisions are less destructive in the marketplace. Many people we engage with may never attend our churches, so our church affiliation isn't as important as an authentic Christian witness.

Everything gets funded from the marketplace. The marketplace shouldn't just be considered "the economic engine of the church." Instead, we should approach it as the largest mission field because it encompasses the world.

The transformative power of marketplace ministry lies in its ability to bring God's kingdom values into everyday business operations. This not only impacts the immediate business environment but also has a ripple effect on the broader community and society.

Model influence and leadership. Christian business leaders can influence industry standards and practices by modeling ethical behavior and advocating for policies that promote justice and equity.

Embrace innovation and creativity. Being open to divine inspiration can lead to innovative solutions that address real-world problems. This positions Christian businesses as leaders in their fields, offering products and services that improve lives.

Lean into Christian testimony and witness. A business that operates on biblical principles becomes a powerful testimony to the transformative power of the gospel. It shows that faith is not just a private matter but has real-world implications for how we live and work.

Develop a biblical worldview. Ground your actions and decisions in a solid understanding of biblical principles.

Regular study of Scripture and prayer can help you align your work with God's purposes.

Build relationships. Establish meaningful connections with colleagues, clients, and customers. Genuine relationships provide opportunities to share your faith and demonstrate God's love.

Exemplify integrity. Let your actions reflect your faith. Consistent ethical behavior and excellence in your work will earn the respect of others and open doors for ministry.

Serve the community. Look for ways to contribute positively to your community. Whether through charitable giving, volunteering, or mentoring, your efforts can make a significant impact.

Seek God's guidance. Regularly seek God's wisdom in your business decisions. "If any of you lacks wisdom, you should ask God, who gives generously to all without finding fault, and it will be given to you."[8]

Ministry in the marketplace is a critical aspect of fulfilling the Great Commission. By integrating faith with daily work and interactions, we can influence the world. The five-fold ministry equips us for this task, while Jesus' example provides a blueprint for effective marketplace engagement. Through demonstrating integrity, excellence, and compassion in our professional lives, we can be powerful witnesses for Christ.

Ministering in the marketplace is a divine calling that integrates faith and work, recognizing the value of each believer's vocation. By following Jesus' example and embracing the diverse gifts within the body of Christ, we can effectively witness to the world.

Jesus' example of ministering in the marketplace underscores the importance of being present and accessible. His compassion for the crowds and his ability to connect with people from all walks of life highlight the necessity of engaging with people where they are. By following His lead, we can touch the lives of those we encounter, no matter where we meet them.

Our work is not merely about professional success but about embodying the fruit of the Spirit and shining our light in dark places. It is through our actions and work ethic that we become witnesses to God's transformative power. As we navigate our careers and daily responsibilities, we should seek opportunities to disciple others, showing them the love and truth of Christ through our example.

Chapter Three

Creation Theology

From the beginning, man was created and purposed to be the representative and representation of God in the earth. But before we can take our rightful place, we must understand God's original intentions, which are rooted in the theology of creation. We can't fulfill God's will or effectively represent Him when we aren't clear on His will and purpose for us.

As believers, we must understand our role as the masterpiece of an omnipotent Creator. Creation theology, therefore, emerges as a critical discipline that seeks to unravel the mysteries of our existence by exploring the divine act of creation as narrated in Genesis 1–3.

Humanity was created in God's image and likeness, and how we represent our Creator influences our work and purpose. By reflecting on God's original design for us, we can better appreciate our pivotal role in God's creation and strive to fulfill His divine mandate as His representative in the earth.

Creation Theology

For centuries, mankind has been fascinated with where we came from, if there is an omnipotent creator with a grand design, and how to figure out our life's purpose.

Our curiosity about our creation is at the same time philosophical, theological, and genealogical. A common starting point for Christians discussing the beginning of humanity and the universe is the Book of Genesis. As believers, we acknowledge the one true God as our Creator, and we recognize a theology of creation that gives us some of the answers we seek. Though we know that mysteries still exist and are God's prerogative to conceal or reveal, God's Word gives us enough information to know who created us and why.

Most of us know that it all began with "In the beginning. . . ." But have we ever done a deep study of what that says about God and our place in His plan for the world? And how does God's actions in creation inform everything else we believe? As we seek answers, we want to look at God's starring role in the created order through the lens of faith in a God who is transcendent and eternal, but who made man and then put him in an elevated position above everything else He created.

Creation theology is more than simply recounting how the world came into being; it is a profound exploration of God's nature, His intentions for humanity, and our place within His grand design. Creation reveals a sequence of divine actions that transformed chaos into order, culminating in the creation of humanity. It offers insights into God's attributes and highlights the special role humans play as His image-bearers and stewards of the earth.

The opening chapters of Genesis serve as the cornerstone for creation theology. These chapters give us foundational truths about our relationship with God and the world. It helps us understand that creation was not a random act but a deliberate, purposeful design by a sovereign God who desires a meaningful relationship with His creation.

Creation theology was put forth by Dr. Don Carson, president and co-founder of The Gospel Coalition and emeritus professor at Trinity Evangelical Divinity School. Dr. Carson forgoes exploring the usual discussions and disagreements surrounding creation, and for now, we should also put those aside. The study of our origins is not just an academic exercise but a spiritual endeavor that draws us closer to the Creator. Understanding God's call to us to work is so crucial to our purpose, that to get bogged down in debates over young earth vs. old earth and evolution isn't helpful but might be an area we can consider at another time.

Dr. Carson identified 12 major themes in Genesis 1–3, but for our study, we will examine six of those themes:[1]

- **God comes first.** Before anything was made, God existed. He's an infinite God with no beginning or end, making Him the supreme Sovereign. He exists in eternity, so He has always been and forever will be. He created all things, so He is self-existent and independent, which means He is independent of His creation.

God's preeminence is the foundation of everything we believe about the created world and ourselves.

- **God speaks.** Genesis 1 says that in the beginning, God created. How did He create? He spoke: "God said, . . ." and everything that was created came forth.[a] God is a talking God whose word is all-powerful but is still accessible to human beings. The Bible says He watches over His word "to perform it,"[b] so God's words are not empty and meaningless. When He speaks, His words are more powerful than our actions. His word is eternal from everlasting to everlasting, and everything God says endures.

- **God works.** When God created the universe, He worked for six days. On the seventh day, He rested. Creation serves as a template for us for work and rest. When we explore the power and purpose of work, we do so recognizing that God requires us to work. It's not an option, and it's not part-time. God's intention from the beginning was that man would work (till the ground) and have dominion over the earth.

- **God created everything (*ex nihilo*: "out of nothing").** "All things were made by him; and without him was not any thing made that was made."[c] God's work is prolific, resulting in the creation of everything that was made, including mankind. God's creation of everything isn't limited to the six days we read about in Genesis and relegated to the past. Everything needed to create anything in the future already existed because God already created it. God created everything out of nothing and has called us to co-create with Him through our own creative and innovative instincts given to us by God.

- **Everything that God created is good.** Genesis 1 walks us through God's creative process. When He spoke, the created order came forth, and He called it good.[d] The word *good* is used to express several nuances of that which is good such as "agreeable," "excellent," and "beneficial." Everything God created has an established purpose and is beneficial in some way to His vast universe. When He created man, the capstone of all His creation, He looked back at all He had created and declared them very good. When God approbates something as good, this means that the thing is functioning as it is intended to function, and it is harmonizing with God's will and purpose. According to *The Wycliffe Bible Encyclopedia*, "God is the standard of all that is good; all that God plans, does, creates, and commands is good. He is the norm, judge and decider of what is good."[2] So things are good only to the extent that they are in harmony with God.

- **Man is the crown jewel of creation.** God created man in His image and likeness, which is not the case for anything else God created. He also made us three-part beings—body, soul, and spirit. No other creature has a soul, which puts us at the top of the hierarchy of creation. Because of our vaulted position, God has made us His representatives or vice-regents and given us our own territory: earth. While God rules in heaven, he has given man dominion over the earth and works through us to achieve His will here. This is at the very heart of our purpose and work.

As God's masterpiece in creation, we bear His image and likeness. The way many of us live shows that we often forget that. So if we are to take our rightful place as vice-regents and co-creators with God, we must understand what it means to be created in His image and likeness and how important that is for our work.

Engaging with creation theology allows us to deepen our understanding of God's intentions and our purpose. It helps us see our lives within the broader context of God's eternal plan. Recognizing that we are created in God's image empowers us to live out our roles as His representatives on earth, fulfilling the mandate to steward and cultivate the resources we've been given.

Divine Resemblance

Physical resemblances mark us as belonging to certain families that give us unique features. Do we look more like our mother's side of the family, or do we favor our father's side? Maybe we resemble our family members more in personality or mannerisms. Perhaps we've inherited traits we're proud to point out and others we'd rather hide. This exploration of identity and resemblance, however, transcends mere physicality when we consider our spiritual lineage as part of God's family.

In the Christian faith, we are called to embody the likeness of our heavenly Father, a likeness not rooted in physical features but in spiritual attributes derived from God's image. As described in Genesis, God formed humanity from the dust of the ground, breathing life into man to create a living soul. This divine breath, or *pneuma*, signifies the unique connection between God's Spirit and the human spirit.

This spiritual connection endows humanity with the ability to bear God's image and likeness, positioning them as representatives, ambassadors, and co-creators on earth. In the garden of Eden, this divine likeness facilitated a harmonious relationship between God and man, illustrated by God's collaborative act of naming the animals with Adam. However, the Fall disrupted this divine resemblance, leading to a loss of innocence and identity and a newfound awareness of nakedness, symbolizing a separation from God's glory.

Thus, our journey of faith involves reclaiming and reflecting this divine image, striving to embody the traits and attributes bestowed on us by our Creator. This spiritual resemblance to God calls us to live out our roles as His representatives, exercising dominion and steward-ship over the earth while reflecting His glory in our lives.

In the family of God, we should look like our heav-enly Father, who in creation gave us His divine image and likeness. In Him, there are no features or traits we should want to hide. Instead, His traits more than our physical features are a point of pride that we should want to be on display all the time. How did we get such traits from God our Father?

"In the beginning. . . ." The word *image* (*selem*) means "copy." *Likeness* (*demut*) means "pattern," "model," or "to function like." At creation, God gave us His image (*imago Dei*, Latin, "image of God"). God is a spirit, so humans didn't inherit God's physical features. Instead, God imprinted on human nature internal and external characteristics that resemble His.

God has many characteristics that are His alone that in our humanness, we can't obtain. For example, God is all-knowing, all-powerful, unchanging, transcendent, eternal, independent, and infinite. However, in making us in His image, God has shared characteristics such as resource-fulness, wisdom, holiness, faithfulness, creativity, mercy, patience, justice, righteousness, wrath, grace, love, good-ness, truthfulness, kindness, and jealousy.[3]

The wonderful news is that every human can share these divine characteristics in some form. That might not look the same or be manifested in every person, but God has not withheld these special traits from us because He created us to be equal in dignity, value, and worth, and God's creative genius is in every one of us.

Since we are patterned after God's likeness, like Him, we can call "those things which be not as though they were."[f] The God who speaks did this in creation: He called for light, sky, creatures, and vegetation where none had existed before. So now we can function like God does when "we walk by faith, not by sight."[g] We don't have to be afraid because God doesn't fear. Fear is a malfunction of God's likeness.

"And the LORD God formed man of the dust of the ground, and breathed into his nostrils the breath of life; and man became a living soul."[h] When man was merely dust on the ground, God looked into eternity and saw what man would become. He took dust, one of the lowest materials, and formed man by creating his body.[i] Then God breathed into man's nostrils "the breath of life" or *pneuma*, which means "spirit."

Although God formed man, it wasn't until He breathed into man the breath of life that man had a connection with God's Spirit. Our souls, then, contain our intellect, emotion, and will.[j] Thus, man became a trichotomous being, consisting of body, soul, and spirit.

Because of *pneuma*, humans are the only beings to have souls, which sets us apart from the dichotomous (body and mind) animals God created. Some people may argue that animals or other created beings have souls, but God didn't breathe life into any other creatures. When God created humans and animals, He made a vast distinction. Humans, with our souls connected to God's breath or Spirit, were created in alignment with God in a significant way, and that unique connection prepares us to be able to bear God's image and likeness.

Likeness means "to resemble someone in action and appearance." When the Bible talks about *image* in this context, it means we resemble and represent God. Part of God's original design makes us representative figures who resemble God, who then allows us to stand in for Him in the earth. We become ambassadors, vice-regents, and co-creators for Him. This exalted position gives us the necessary authority to rule over and have dominion over the territory God has assigned us.

In the garden of Eden, God had a harmonious connection with man. The Bible tells us that God created the animals and then collaborated with Adam on what to name them. Since God is the Creator, why didn't He name them? By collaborating with Adam, God was establishing a precedent of leadership in man and delineating man's territory, or where he would be expected to have dominion.

After Adam and Eve disobeyed God, they lost their divine likeness and perceived themselves to be naked and void of God's glory. When God came to visit with Adam in the garden, Adam was nowhere to be found. God called out to Adam, "Where are you?" Adam explained that he was in hiding because he had discovered his nakedness. He went from being the alpha male on the planet clothed in the image of God to hiding out in obscurity. Before the Fall, even the animals likely would have bowed to Adam because they could see God's likeness in man and wouldn't have dared to attack or harm him.

In the aftermath of the Fall, humanity's divine resemblance was marred yet not entirely lost. The innate connection to God, the potential to reflect His glory, and the call to dominion remained but required restoration. Through the redemption offered by Christ, the pathway to regaining our divine resemblance was revealed. By embracing this restoration, we are called once again to embody the image and likeness of God, displaying His attributes in our lives and interactions.

This divine resemblance is more than mere appearance; it is reflected in our actions, thoughts, and relationships. It calls us to live with purpose, exercising stewardship over creation, demonstrating love and compassion, and seeking justice and righteousness. This is why Christ commanded us to be holy. In doing so, we fulfill our role as God's representatives, bringing His kingdom into clearer focus for all to see.

Our physical and spiritual resemblances shape our identity and purpose. While our earthly lineage connects us to our families, our divine lineage calls us to a higher standard. By nurturing our relationship with God and aligning our lives with His will, we can fully realize and display the divine image in which we were created, living as true children of our heavenly Father.

The Search for Fulfillment

As a result of the Fall, man lost his intimate connection with God. From that day to this, we struggle to be in right relationship with our Creator and be an effective representation in the world. That disconnection creates a void that has set man on various paths in search of God, gods, or other supernatural beings. This is the essence of all religions: a search for supernatural powers. This search has led many people down the rabbit hole of multiple religions that leads to no connection with God.

God created us for connection, so if we don't connect with the God of all creation, we will connect to something else. True fulfillment can only be achieved through our connection with Christ, who brings us back in alignment with the image and likeness of God.

Without a connection to God, we have an inherent identity crisis,[k] and we naturally gravitate toward other influences to find our identity, whether they are other gods, movements, or religions. Our environment shapes us, and in the absence of divine guidance, we derive our identity from our surroundings, striving for relevance through cultural assimilation.

This disconnection subjects us to the control of our human senses and the influences of others, limiting our responses to stimuli from the physical world. So the only way to get relevance is to attach to the culture around us. But these replacements are mere shadows of the true connection we were designed for, leading us to form identities influenced heavily by our surroundings rather than our inherent divine nature.

When we are disconnected from God, we are ruled by our human senses or that of other people. Our senses then inform our souls—the intellect, emotions, and decision component—which respond to stimuli from the five physical senses. In our disconnected state, we are controlled only by the things we can touch, taste, see, hear, and smell. Without God, we can only react or respond to the things that happen in the physical or earthly realm.

But God ordained us to be His vice-regents, and a vice-regent disconnected from God can only operate in dysfunction and make crucial mistakes. To illustrate, imagine being an ambassador for the United States to a foreign country. Your role is to represent the interests of the United States and its government. If you fail to maintain regular communication with the president and government officials back home, you will soon be out of touch with vital information and unable to fulfill your duties effectively.

Your actions would no longer represent your country's interests but your own, which can be perilous. First, it's dangerous because we're not empowered to operate under our own power. Second, depending on the relationship between the United States and the other country, your role as an ambassador may be the difference between saving American lives or losing them. That's how important your role may be.

Similarly, as God's vice-regents in the earth, our effectiveness is contingent upon God regularly infusing us and downloading into us new and relevant information. We haven't been named vice-regents to be self-important. We haven't been given resources, skills, talents, and abilities to hoard them for ourselves. We have been divinely placed as vice-regents bearing God's image so that we can help save others. Our influence, if we use it appropriately, may be the difference between souls being saved or lost.

The longer we remain disconnected, the further we are from God. God is always active and working, and He will work through those who are determined to stay connected to Him. If we're not in right relationship, we will be stuck and ineffective. As God's vice-regents, our role is crucial and requires a continuous connection with Him. Just as ambassadors must stay in regular contact with their home countries to effectively represent their interests, we too must remain connected to God to fulfill our divine purpose. When we establish a connection with God, we're made alive,[l] we are renewed,[m] and we know who we are.[n]

God

Spirit

Soul

Body

<u>**Gen. 2:17 (NKJV)**</u>
"...for the day you eat of it you shall surely die"

<u>**Eph 2:1b (NKJV)**</u>
"...You were dead in trespasses sin in which you once walk in the course of this world..."

<u>**Soul**</u>
Mind, Emotion, Will

<u>**Five Physical Senses**</u>
See, Hear, Touch, Smell, Taste

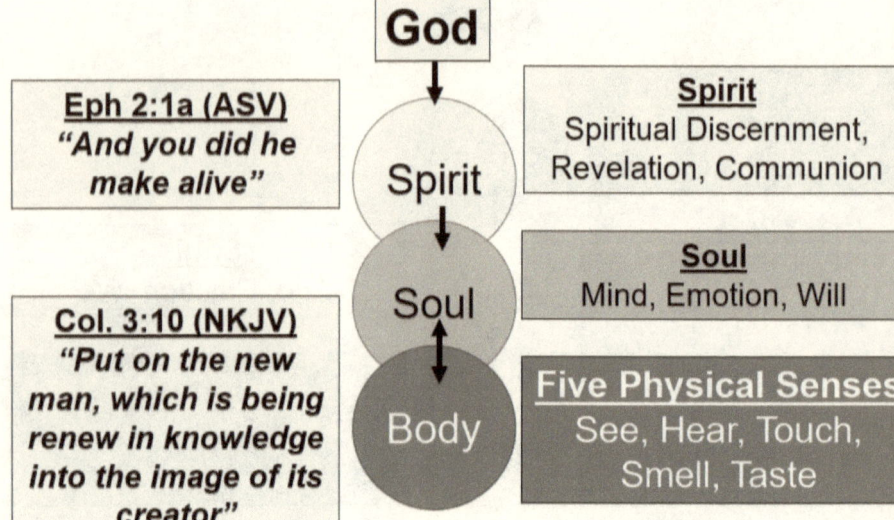

God

Spirit

Soul

Body

Eph 2:1a (ASV)
"And you did he make alive"

Col. 3:10 (NKJV)
"Put on the new man, which is being renew in knowledge into the image of its creator"

Spirit
Spiritual Discernment, Revelation, Communion

Soul
Mind, Emotion, Will

Five Physical Senses
See, Hear, Touch, Smell, Taste

By using the theology of creation as our point of reference, we begin to understand the foundational truths about our relationship with God and the world. We will also understand God's redemptive plan to use us in the marketplace to reconcile the world to Himself and to bring His creation back to its original design for humanity.

God's Likeness and Image in the Marketplace

Often, I ask college students, "What are you going to do when you graduate?" The modern age presents many possibilities to young people—traveling, embarking on personal quests for self-discovery, or diving headfirst into professional careers. I remind them, though, that they should start with the Creator. I tell them to seek Him and find out what He wants.

God created us with purpose, so it's our responsibility to find that purpose. It's important to help steer young people in the right direction because they're looking for someone to relate to, for something to give them purpose, but they're often missing it because no one is encouraging them to connect to God.

When we are not in alignment with God's purpose for us, we find ourselves assimilating with what's around us, taking cues from a worldly culture that leaves us dead to our God-given purpose, following the course and fashion of the world, and succumbing to the power of the age. These consequences underscore the pitfalls of conforming to worldly standards and neglecting the spiritual dimension of our existence. When disconnected from God's purpose, we succumb to the desires and dictates of the flesh, which ultimately lead us astray.

Although God has commissioned us to represent Him in the marketplace, our mandate isn't to "churchify" everything or shove the Bible in people's faces. Instead, God wants us to make real and meaningful connections with people and point them to Him. To fulfill this mandate, we must embrace God's original design for humanity. This design calls for us to be beacons of His love and truth, reflecting His character in our lives. It's about demonstrating integrity, compassion, and excellence in all we do, thereby drawing others toward God's light within us.

As young people venture into the next phases of their lives, it is imperative to ground them in this truth. They need to understand that their ultimate purpose is not in pursuing worldly accolades but in aligning themselves with God's will. Encouraging them to seek divine guidance will not only steer them toward fulfilling their God-given potential but also equip them positively to impact the world around them.

The journey of discovering divine purpose begins with seeking the Creator. We need to see beyond the transient allure of cultural norms and find enduring fulfillment in our relationship with God. By doing so, we are empowered to live lives of significance and purpose, grounded in the unwavering foundation of the truth of God's Word.

The search for fulfillment highlights the inherent void left by our disconnection from God. This disconnection drives us to seek identity and purpose from external sources. However, reconnecting with God restores our true identity and empowers us to fulfill our divine mandate. Our effectiveness as God's vice-regents hinges on this continuous connection, enabling us to operate under divine guidance and influence.

Physical and spiritual resemblance is a profound metaphor for our identity and purpose. Just as we inherit physical traits from our earthly families, we bear the divine image and likeness of our heavenly Father. This spiritual resemblance calls us to a higher standard, urging us to live out our roles as representatives and co-creators with authority and dominion over the earth.

Genesis 1–3 gives us valuable insights into God's pre-eminence, the power of His Word, the template of work and rest, the comprehensive nature of God's creation, the inherent goodness of all He created, and humanity's exalted position as the crown jewel of the divine order. By understanding the profound truths embedded in the act of creation, we can better appreciate our place in the divine order and our purpose in God's magnificent plan. God desires that we see more clearly His image within us and strive to reflect His glory in the marketplace.

Chapter Four

Restoration of the Image of God

From the beginning, God's design for humanity involved work, dominion, and stewardship. The biblical narrative illustrates an ideal state where humanity lived in perfect harmony with God, one another, and the natural world. But the fall of humanity introduced a deviation from God's original design, leading to a world marked by fear, abuse, and a misunderstanding of purpose.

However, God, in His omniscience, prepared a plan for redemption through Jesus Christ, aiming to reconcile us to His original intent. Everything God has done since man's expulsion from the garden of Eden has been to restore mankind to Himself.

Servant leadership, as modeled by Jesus, contradicts worldly views of leadership characterized by power and dominance. Instead, it emphasizes humility, service, and uplifting others. This approach challenges leaders to reassess their motivations and methods, ensuring that their actions are aligned with the principles of serving and stewarding God's creation.

Jesus demonstrated the prerequisite for kingdom leadership when He washed His disciples' feet.[a] He performed this act of service because His Father had placed all things under His authority.[b] Later, He told His disciples to mirror the example that He had set.[c] When Jesus washed the disciples' feet, it wasn't about cleanliness because He later told Peter that he did not need cleansing; rather, he needed humility to lead.

I counsel leaders in churches and workplaces that the path of leadership is humility, and nothing else is more important. Service is oxymoronic to the arrogant and the proud, but to servant leaders, it is their roadmap to greatness. As we wrestle with the complexities of leadership in a broken world, our ultimate goal is to align our actions with God's heavenly mandates. By embracing the model of servant leadership, we can create environments where everyone can be restored to the image of God.

Created for Dominion

God created us for purpose and work. That's why for most of us our church buildings are not our primary mission field. Instead, God has called us as vice-regents to represent Him in the marketplace, outside the insular walls of our churches. God has given us the whole world to win, so we must broaden our thinking to match the vastness of our territory. The work God has assigned us has many facets, and we must understand what they are.

Before God created man, no shrub or vegetation grew in the garden of Eden[d] because there was no man to till the ground. The word *till* means "to work," "to serve," and "to worship." So it was God-intended that no matter the job, occupation, profession, or career, at the heart of it is the mandate to worship God and to serve others. If we don't approach our work with the desire to worship and serve, then our work is vanity and does not honor and glorify God in any way.

When God assigned man to work, He gave man his own territory: the earth. The psalmist wrote, "The heaven, even the heavens, are the LORD's: but the earth hath given he to the children of men."[e] Everything that happens on the earth becomes a collaboration between God and man because man is a co-creator with God. "Every plant of the field before it was in the earth, and every herb of the field before it grew: for the LORD God had not caused it to rain upon the earth, and there was not a man to till the ground."[f] As vice-regent on earth, man has a unique partnership and collaboration with God as we work synergistically to align what happens on earth with what God intends in heaven.

Jesus told His disciples, "Whatsoever ye shall bind on earth shall be bound in heaven: and whatsoever ye shall loose on earth shall be loosed in heaven."[g] Scripture shows that it's our responsibility to bring what happens on earth as close to God's heavenly mandates as possible, not the other way around. Jesus also taught His disciples to pray, "Your kingdom come, Your will be done on earth as it is in heaven."[h]

How does God's kingdom come to earth? The only way that can happen is for us to "give God permission" to exercise authority in the earth. To some people, that statement might sound like sacrilege, but let's explore what it means.

As the Creator and CEO of all creation, God wants us to exercise dominion and not be vice-regents in name only. So when God wants something to happen on earth, He chooses to work through human agency to accomplish it. God could have chosen to work through angels, but that wasn't His plan. Even when man needed salvation, God sent a man, Jesus, to redeem us back to Himself. That was His design, and He doesn't go against His design.

God then gave man dominion over this territory. "God blessed them, and God said unto them, Be fruitful, and multiply, and replenish the earth, and subdue it: and have dominion over the fish of the sea, and over the fowl of the air, and over every living thing that moveth upon the earth."[i] To "replenish the earth" isn't about filling it again. God's mandate to us is that the manifestation of anything, of any present reality, is man's responsibility.

Dominion (*radah*) "means to lead, direct, manage, rule, dominate, prevail." God never defined *dominion* as "to abuse, misuse, or waste." Man's responsibility is to care for and steward the resources under his dominion. Another aspect of our dominion is the importance of being created in God's image and likeness. We can't stand in the place of a sovereign God without properly representing God and reflecting Him in our world.

Within that dominion is the power to manifest or to produce. The manifestation of dominion transcends material possessions, although sometimes there may be tangible things that result. When we try to "manifest" cars, houses, vacations, marriages, and money just to stockpile them for our own use, we will miss the greater purpose for which we are called. This contemporary concept of "manifest" will cause us to live in frustration, disappointment, and emptiness. It will lead us to question our faith, our salvation, and our walk with God.

Unfortunately, the next steps after disappointment are anger and confusion directed toward God because we begin to believe He didn't come through for us and give us what we wanted. What I'm encouraging you to realize is that God called you to co-create with Him, to till the ground, which means to improve the conditions around you. That is manifestation, which is a result of aligning our mindsets, hearts, and spirits with God's will and work instead of trying to get God to align with our wills.

For Adam, the manifestation of his dominion was the fruit of his labor. When he tilled the ground, he produced that which had not existed before. Setting the context for dominion, God made man the vice-regent of all creation. God chose man, His crown jewel, to oversee everything God created, so our dominion is a divine mandate, giving man the power to represent God in all that will be created and produced in the future.

God's Mandate: Be Productive!

At creation, God gave humans the mandate to be fruitful, multiply, replenish, and subdue the earth.[j] God's concept of fruitfulness here does not refer just to childbearing, though that is certainly one component of it. Rather, in the broader context, it is referring to productivity. Jesus did not have children, but He was productive. Paul did not have children, but he was productive. God wants us to continue to be productive until we fill the earth, which is still God's mandate to humanity today.

John wrote about Jesus' interpretation of that mandate in practical terms while he was on earth.[k] Jesus said that His Father is the Gardner, and He is the Branch. The Gardner cuts off every branch that bears no fruit, while every branch that does bear fruit, He prunes so that it will be even more fruitful.

In church or in the marketplace, it is the leader's responsibility to ensure productivity among his staff. If members of my staff are unproductive, I must assess whether the issue is a lack of training, resources, talent, or passion. It is my responsibility to bring the proper resources and training to help my team members become more productive.

If after all those things have been done those team members remain unproductive, then they should be coached to look for something else that best fits their giftings and skills. However, if those team members are productive, it's the leader's responsibility to continue cultivating the gifts to enable them to do more.

A Call to Authentic Leadership

According to writer and pastor John Maxwell, "leadership is influence."[1] God created everyone with the ability to have influence and offer it as a benefit to others. You don't have to have a title, be rich, or have the power to lead because we're all created to lead. The question isn't, "Are you a leader?" We should ask, "How are you using your influence? Are you benefiting other people or harming them?"

After the Fall, mankind found itself in a broken, sinful, corrupt, and demoralizing world, which gave rise to leaders who became dictators, despots, crooks, murderers, and thieves. The Bible warns us of this, so we shouldn't be surprised.

Many corrupt leaders are operating out of fear. Instead of using their influence to bring people and resources together to benefit the world, these corrupt leaders desire to control and dominate people, break their spirits, line their own pockets, and maintain power. Those leadership styles are inconsistent with what God intended since fear is a malfunction of God's original design.

In the garden, God established man's origins to work and to have dominion, and how we do that matters. The style of leadership we choose will make or break us. Jesus said, "Not so shall it be among you; but whoever wishes to be great among you must be your servant, and whoever desires to be first among you must be your slave—Just as the Son of Man came not to be waited on but to serve, and to give His life as a ransom for many [the price paid to set them free."[1]

This Scripture gives Jesus' endorsement for servant leadership, which He modeled among His disciples. Servant leadership contradicts the worldly view of leadership. It calls for humility, service, and a focus on benefiting others rather than seeking personal gain or dominance.

In a world where leadership is often equated with power and authority, servant leadership offers a refreshing and transformative perspective. Rooted in biblical principles, this approach emphasizes serving others, stewarding resources, and aligning one's work with God's will. Church and corporate leaders claim to be servant leaders, but many don't understand what that means. If they did, then the way they pastor, treat their employees, or approach their work would have to shift.

Servant leadership is incongruent with "lording over" people, having dictatorial tendencies that would be abusive, or wanting others to serve and wait on us. Our giftings are meant to benefit others, so we should lean into offering those giftings at every opportunity to everyone.

This approach challenges leaders to reassess their motivations and methods, ensuring that their actions are aligned with the principles of serving and uplifting others. It underscores the importance of integrity, compassion, and the willingness to work collaboratively to achieve a greater purpose. Ultimately, servant leadership is about co-creating with God and manifesting His kingdom on earth through our everyday actions and decisions.

God created man and said it was good or beneficial. How are we benefiting one another? How are we benefiting the world? Our giftedness and purpose are what we have to offer. If we're serving up our gift, then we're benefitting others. As leaders, we don't seek to be served or waited on. Instead, we must seek to serve and benefit others.

It's our responsibility to find the resources needed, create vision, and serve others by bringing people and resources together to get the job done. Serving others also includes developing people, helping others cultivate their gifts, and not just being concerned with enriching ourselves. Servant leadership may seem counterintuitive and might not make sense to those who believe leadership is about exercising power and authority over people and acquiring as many possessions as possible. But servant leadership works, and it works for all people at all levels.

When my wife, Kim, and I were working on a big project, we assembled the people and resources we needed to get the job done. Leaders are like conductors who stand before an orchestra waving their batons this way and that, making sure the sounds of the various musicians are on time and harmonious and result in a beautiful, mellifluous masterpiece.

Leaders are responsible for bringing resources, abilities, skills, and giftings into a harmonious whole. Then we create a vision for what it would look like and help people cultivate their giftings. We regularly ask, "What more do you need?" Whatever their answer, my response to them is, "OK, let's figure out how to get it. Let's go get that."

A perfect example of a microcosm of leadership is marriage. The two people in the couple are co-equal. One sits in a position of headship and has the vision, but it's just a role within the home. It's not meant to be an excuse to be abusive. God has given the head of the household the responsibility for creating the vision just as a pastor creates the vision for the church. If there is no one in a position of headship, that leaves a leadership vacuum, which leaves room for chaos. The reason God is not against hierarchy is because it offers structure and order and lessens the opportunity for chaos.

Just as in marriage, we should never use our positions to dominate or abuse other people. We have dominion over the earth's resources, and we are supposed to bring those together with the people who need them. But that's where our dominion ends because we're never to dominate or lord over people since we're not superior to anyone.

We are all servants to one another and to God. Only God is superior and supreme. We're exercising dominion within the framework of the Fall, man's sin of disobedience in the garden of Eden. Everything we see that's opposed to God's original design is informed by that fact.

"Neither as being lords over God's heritage, but being examples to the flock."[m] We care by watching over them, not because we must, but because we are willing. We're also not pursuing dishonest gain, but we're eager to serve. Kingdom leadership is leading by kingdom precepts and principles and is the reverse of what the world values. The leadership of this world lifts up the elite and the well-connected into places of power, and they don't always serve others. Instead, they wait to be served.

Jesus promoted kingdom principles, which make room for everyone to lead and have something valuable to offer, and everyone serves and is served. "Not lording it over those entrusted to you, but being examples to the flock."[n] God isn't against hierarchy, but He is against abuses of power over other people. So the idea of leadership is not about lording over people but leading by example and leading with compassion.

Some people are not called to certain positions. They are promoted to them. When people are promoted but not called, they will lead from a base of fear because they worry they may lose their positions. They're insecure and afraid they'll be seen as frauds. They'll lose power, position, control, and authority, so they must dominate people and resources instead of unifying people with resources and developing people and their potential. God doesn't want us to pursue dishonest gain but to be eager to serve.

Be forewarned. Leadership isn't always easy. John and James's mother went to Jesus and asked Him to promote her sons, to place one on Jesus' right and the other on the left.º Jesus challenged her by asking if James and John could drink from the same cup or be baptized with the same baptism.

To follow Christ, we will suffer. Some believers are physically persecuted, and others are shunned, canceled, and stripped of a platform to speak. But when we're walking in God's path for us, He is with us through it all.

Restoration of the Image of God

The fall of humanity marked a significant turning point in the relationship between God and man. This disconnection has had a profound ripple effect that has reverberated through time, shaping our existence and struggles to reconnect with our Creator. Being restored to God's image and likeness required the sacrificial death of the Son of God, Jesus Christ. On our part, it means accepting that sacrifice and being committed to our purpose.

Historically, God works in periods called "dispensations." In every dispensation, God uses different methods to bring man back to Himself by providing what man needs to be faithful and obedient. However, in every age, man has failed. When the methods in one dispensation didn't work, God used another method in the next dispensation.

Before the Fall was the dispensation of innocence. Following that were the dispensations of conscience, human government, promise, and law. Today, we live in the dispensation of grace, the church age. God is now using the church as another vehicle in this period to save man and bring us to Christ. The church isn't a building or a physical structure where we gather to worship. The church (the *ekklesia*, the called-out ones) is a group of people bound together by a common commitment to bear witness of Christ to the world.

In this period, as we live under the protection of God's grace, which is the power to do what we can't do ourselves, we are called upon to grant grace to others who may not always get it right. Since we are not perfect, we should give others permission to be imperfect in our lives. Even though God's power works in and through us, we will not reach perfection until we see God face-to-face in the dispensation of the millennial kingdom of Christ.

Until then, God has made provisions for our forgiveness once and for all. As He hung on the cross, He said, "Father, forgive them." He wasn't just talking about those persons who stood at the foot of the cross watching His crucifixion. Rather, He was talking about all of mankind.

Although the church age is firmly planted in the dispensation of grace, we tend to want to teeter back and forth from law to grace and use the law as our measuring stick for how holy we are supposed to live. We take on a spirit of legalism that God has not mandated. Jesus became sin for us in the "great exchange" so that we might be righteous before God through Christ. Paul had much zeal concerning the law, which is why he participated in persecuting the saints. He struggled with legalism and grace until he met Jesus on the road to Damascus.

To avoid legalism, we must reorient our minds so that we see ourselves, and help others see themselves, as vice-regents. We are co-creators. We are image-bearers of God, the sovereign God of the universe, so we represent him in the earth. Along with being named vice-regent comes the power to manifest or to produce. Through that, God's glory is revealed.

The journey of humanity through various dispensations reflects God's unwavering commitment to bring us back to Him. The dispensation of grace offers a unique opportunity for mankind to embrace forgiveness and grace through Jesus Christ. During this period, our challenge is to resist the pull of legalism and fully embrace and extend grace, moving away from legalism and toward a collaborative, creative partnership with God, transforming our lives and interactions with others. In doing so, we align ourselves with God's ultimate plan of restoration, moving ever closer to the perfection that will be realized in the millennial kingdom of Christ.

God's Original Design

Humanity lost its way and moved away from God's original design for us. This divergence prompts the question, What is God's original design, and is it still possible to return to that? By examining the biblical narrative and understanding the implications of straying from our intended purpose, we can gain insight into how we might realign ourselves with this original design.

This initial state can be likened to an engineer's design process. When designing a product, an engineer regularly thinks about the "why." *Why am I designing this? What is its original function?* The engineer has a specific purpose in mind, ensuring that the product functions optimally within its intended parameters. Using a phone as an analogy, it is designed for communication, internet browsing, and running applications, not as a hammer or a scrub brush. Using the phone outside its intended purpose will make it inoperable. Similarly, humanity's deviation from God's original purpose leads to various forms of dysfunction and brokenness.

In the garden of Eden, Adam and Eve lived naked without shame, completely transparent with each other and

God. They interacted harmoniously with animals, exercising dominion over them without fear. Adam, adorned with the glory of God, was fearless because death was not part of the equation. The fear of death, which entered after the Fall, has since been the root of all the fears of humanity's experiences. The fear of death has kept men in bondage throughout their lives.[p] Without death, there would be no fear, and thus, no bondage.

The Bible cautions against domineering behavior, even among parents. Fathers are advised not to frustrate their children by the way they treat them. Rather, they should bring up their children with proper discipline and instruction.[q] We are reminded that children are our heritage,[r] and we are urged to train them in the way they should go, according to God's purpose for their lives.[s]

Parents should be stewards, helping their children discover their unique purposes in God's design rather than molding them into cookie-cutter images of themselves. We should help them to understand that they're uniquely created to do something uncommon in the earth. We may not know what that is, but we should create a conducive atmosphere for them to discover God's purpose for themselves.

We must not resign ourselves to the brokenness of the world. God, in His omniscience, anticipated humanity's fall and prepared a plan for redemption through Jesus Christ. This plan aims to reconcile us with God, restoring us to His original design. Christ is the Lamb slain from the foundation of the world,[t] and God's plan for reconciliation was established before the Fall.

So the way has already been prepared for us to be "reconciled [brought back and reconnected] to God."[u] We will return to the original design because God has ordained it to be so. At the rapture, everything will be restored, and there'll be a new heaven and new earth. We will then coexist the way God intended.

What should we do until that time comes? Jesus told a parable about a nobleman who was going on a journey, but first, he gave his servants the equivalent of "[. . . one hundred days' wages or nearly twenty dollars]."[v] Then he said, "Occupy until I come,"[w] which means that he intended for them to work while he was gone.

God has made us vice-regents and co-creators with Him and intends for us to work, till, serve, lead, worship, and exercise dominion until He returns. All those actions overlap seamlessly and will keep us so busy until the coming of the Lord that we won't have time for anything that isn't included in God's call and mandate on our lives.

Living according to God's original design will often be countercultural. When we display God's design authentically, it draws others to us, prompting them to inquire about the hope within us. This opens doors for genuine conversations about faith. Our lives should speak for us. How we work should speak for us. It doesn't matter if we're janitors or CEOs, people should still see Christ in us without us saying a word.

People should see how we till, work, and serve. We should strive to be the best janitors, nurses, teachers, CEOs, stockbrokers, and postal workers so that people see us and want to know more. When we serve as unto God, somebody somewhere will see our service.

Rediscovering and living according to God's original design is a journey of faith, reflection, and intentionality. By understanding our purpose and aligning our actions with God's plan, we can navigate our lives in a way that honors His design and draws others to Him.

As we wrestle with the challenges of leadership in a broken world, we must remember that our ultimate goal is to align our actions with God's heavenly mandates. By fostering a spirit of cooperation, unity, and mutual respect, we can fulfill our roles as leaders who bring God's kingdom principles to earth. Embracing this servant leadership model will enable us to create a harmonious and productive environment where everyone can thrive and contribute to the greater good.

Humanity's deviation from God's original design has led to a world filled with fear, abuse, and misunderstanding of purpose. Despite this, God has always had a plan to reconcile us to Himself through Jesus Christ. Our mission, until the final restoration, is to live out our lives in a way that reflects God's image and purpose. This involves working diligently, serving others, and living counterculturally in a manner that draws people to the hope within us.

By being authentic in our faith and actions, we can inspire others to seek God's original design for their lives. Ultimately, God's plan for reconciliation and restoration will come to fruition, and we will experience the world as He originally intended.

The narrative of humanity's fall and the subsequent efforts to restore the relationship between God and man underscores the profound impact of this disconnection. Each dispensation, from innocence to law, and now grace, reflects God's persistent attempts to guide humanity back to Him. The ultimate sacrificial act of Jesus Christ serves as the pivotal moment of redemption, offering a path for humanity to reclaim its divine image and purpose.

As believers, the challenge lies in avoiding the pitfalls of legalism and instead embracing our role as co-creators and marketplace leaders, bearing His image and manifesting His glory on earth. By doing so, we fulfill our divine mandate, reflecting God's sovereignty and grace until the day we are perfected in His presence.

Chapter Five

God's Plan for Work

The concept of work has often been viewed as laborious and oppressive, especially in a post-Edenic world where work is often seen as an unavoidable necessity rather than a purposeful endeavor. However, a closer examination of biblical teachings, particularly from the Book of Genesis, reveals a deeper and more noble understanding of work as a form of worship and service to God. From the beginning, God's plan for humanity involved work that is meaningful and co-creative, allowing mankind to manifest God's glory on earth.

Furthermore, the teachings of the apostle Paul in the New Testament show how to successfully manage work in a fallen world, highlighting the importance of maintaining a God-centered perspective on all labor. This approach not only elevates the dignity of work but also aligns it with God's original design, transforming even the most mundane tasks into acts of worship.

We must also consider the challenges of modern work environments, where oppressive leadership and dehumanizing conditions are prevalent. We must push for a paradigm shift from self-preservation to seeking God's direction in our vocational pursuits. By discovering and pursuing our God-given gifts and passions, we can find fulfillment and purpose in our work, trusting that God will provide for our needs as promised in Scripture. We can discover the theological significance of work as outlined in Genesis, the impact of the Fall on our perception of work, and how embracing a divine perspective can transform our approach to labor.

The Original Design of Work

Since the Fall, humanity's relationship with work has long been fraught with a sense of fatigue and drudgery, which is defined as "dull, irksome fatiguing work: uninspiring or menial labor." The average person will spend over 90,000 hours at work.[1] This type of work is often dehumanizing and oppressive, which is why people may resist embracing the beauty and purpose of work. However, God originated work as a noble and divine activity, integral to humanity's purpose and existence. God planned for man to till the ground so he could participate in God's plan to fill the earth with His glory.

The word *till* comes from the Hebrew *abod*, which means "to work," "to serve," and "to worship." God's mandate of work is so important that it is mentioned in the Bible 800 times! When we understand the purpose and importance of work and how it fits into God's original design for us, then we understand why God made us co-creators with Him. When we work, we're also serving, worshiping, and showing God's glory in the earth.

God created everything out of nothing. We are called to co-create from that which has already been created. In other words, God created the trees and called man to create houses and furniture from the trees He created. King Solomon said, "God hath given to the sons of men to be exercised in it. He hath made every thing beautiful in his time: also he hath set the world in their heart, so that no man can find out the work that God maketh from the beginning to the end."[a] Genesis tells us about God's mandate for man to fill and replenish the earth.[b] By working, humans participate in manifesting God's glory. Because God gave us dominion over the earth, we can fulfill that mandate through God's strength.

According to Genesis, God planted a garden and then placed man there. But the plants needed to sustain man didn't immediately blossom because there wasn't anyone to "till the ground."[c] There was also no rain, so none of the cultivated plants could spring up.

To cultivate the vegetation for food, someone would need to till the ground and be responsible for taking care of those plants. That became Adam's job. This labor was not merely a means of survival but an act of worship and obedience to God. Through work, Adam expressed his reverence for God and fulfilled his purpose.

That was Adam's worship and service to the God who had created him. By working, cultivating the plants, and causing them to grow, man was also obeying God's mandate to "be fruitful, and multiply, and replenish the earth, and subdue it: and have dominion over the fish of the sea, and over the fowl of the air, and over every living thing that moveth upon the earth."[d] Adam's obedience in his work was high worship to God and was intended to be a sacred act of obedience and collaboration. Through this lens, work transcends mere labor and becomes a divine partnership in fulfilling God's desire to cultivate and replenish the earth.

As Adam worked in obedience, God came down to collaborate and co-create with him in the cool of the evening. God and man had a significant connection because of God's plan and man's work and obedience. This is the relationship that God longs to have with us, and He always stands ready to receive us back in reconciliation.

The Impact of the Fall

The Fall introduced a distorted view of work, transforming it into a burdensome endeavor. In our post-Fall world, many experience work under dehumanizing conditions, often managed by leaders who fail to recognize the inherent dignity of labor and its sacred connection with God. When we view work as something we do simply to survive, we're looking at it through a carnal framework. We have leaders, CEOs, managers, and supervisors who don't understand how to treat the people they lead. Instead, they rely on leadership styles that lord over or abuse people, disregard everyone's value and worth, and oppress those they should be serving.

In the culture the apostle Paul lived in, slavery was part of life, so much so that it wasn't condemned. But there was a socially acceptable way for masters and their servants to coexist. "Slaves were told to serve well and so glorify Christ." Masters were told that they were accountable to their Master in heaven, which implied that they were not to dehumanize or mistreat their servants.[2]

The Book of Philemon is Paul's letter to Philemon, a master, on behalf of his slave, Onesimus. *Onesimus*, meaning "useful" or "profitable," was a common name for slaves at that time. Although it seems Onesimus had run away, he had been in service with Paul and received Christ. Now, Paul wanted Philemon to receive Onesimus back not only as his slave but as a beloved brother.[2] Paul underscored the need for compassion, and his letter could be a template for all who work and lead to understanding how to treat others with respect and as beloved brothers and sisters in Christ.

Self-Actualization vs. Self-Preservation

To harmonize with God, one must first seek self-actualization over self-preservation. Before the Fall, Adam had a clear sense of who God was, the purpose of his being, and the potential he possessed to accomplish his mandate of dominion. He got up every day, bursting with possibilities, fully expecting each day to bring him one step closer to filling the earth with God's glory, which John Piper defines as "the infinite beauty and splendor of God's manifold perfection."[3] This was what Adam understood his life's purpose to be; this is what he was created to do: fill the earth with the infinite beauty and splendor of God's manifold perfection.

As the heavens showcase God's glory and handiwork,[e] Adam was created and mandated to expand God's glory everywhere he went. However, after being expelled from the garden and having lost the right of dominion, Adam faced each day, not with hopeful expectations, but with persistent dread. Nothing was as easy as it once was. What used to be sweatless work became an arduous and tedious enterprise.

Outside the garden, Adam found himself gripped with fear, reluctant about his future, and hiding from anything that may discover his nakedness and kill him. He worked and gathered enough to sustain himself and his family for another day as he waited in fear of imminent death. This was the beginning of the self-preservation of life or "the survival of the fittest."

Over time, various people realized how far they had fallen from God's original intentions and developed their own relationships with God based on their faith in His plan for their lives despite their present circumstances. By faith, Abel brought a better sacrifice to God than Cain. It was what he believed and not what he brought that made the difference.

By faith, Noah believed the warning about something not yet seen, built a ship in the middle of dry land, and saved his entire household. By faith, Abraham said yes to God's call to travel to an unknown place that would later be his inheritance even though he did not know where he was going.[f]

These men, and many like them, discovered a more meaningful and purpose-driven life through their belief in God rather than a life dominated by the fear of death. Every day, they lived out their God-ordained purpose to fill the earth with the beauty and splendor of God's manifold perfection.

When God called Jeremiah to speak to nations and kingdoms, the young prophet protested in fear because of his age and the perception of those to whom he was called to persuade. God rebuked his fear and reminded him that before he was formed in his mother's womb, God knew him and purposefully ordained and appointed him for his time and generation.

King David, when faced with crushing distress and imminent danger, concluded that in times of great fear are the moments he chose to trust God and His promises for his life. David did not deny his impulses of fear but counteracted those impulses with the confidence of God's protection and the promise of a more fulfilling life.

In essence, David discovered that his faith in God was bigger than his fear.

Jesus ultimately confronted the fears that lead to self-preservation in his teachings on the mount when He admonished His disciples not to worry about what they were going to eat, drink, or wear. Arguably these things are necessary for survival, but Jesus needed to confront the paralyzing, fear-based emotion of worrying about things that are of secondary importance.

Instead, Jesus encouraged them to seek what is of primary importance: their kingdom assignment and purpose. Everything else would fall in place.[g] Seek self-actualization, the attainment of purpose, versus self-preservation, the attainment of things. We should seek what God created us to be, and we will have what God desires us to have.

The Apostle Paul on the Nobility of Work

To reclaim the nobility of work, we must shift our perspective and seek to understand God's original intentions for work. God never intended for work to be arduous or tedious but to fulfill a generational need that is of beneficial service to the world. It was said of King David that after he had served God's purpose in his generation, he fell asleep and was buried with his fathers. This should be the desire of laborers in any capacity: to serve their generation, lay it all out on the field, and die with no regrets.

Paul, in his letter to the Colossians, wrote, "Whatever you do [whatever your task may be] work from the soul, put in your very best effort as something being done for the Lord and not for men."[h] In other words, when our work is done for the Lord and not for men, our motivations will be pure and our energy toward our work will be inexhaustible.

We may live in a post-Fall world, but God's principles of work harmoniously co-exist with the divine purpose of our presence on the planet. So whether we are in positions of authority, or if we report to people in authority, we have a responsibility to work and manage resources as God intended.

Our approach to work matters. Notice that I have not mentioned the word *job* yet because I have been careful to use a word that is more in alignment with God's intention: work. There is a huge difference between a job versus work. My mentor, the late Myles Munroe, made the distinction that a job is what you are trained to do while your work is what you are called to do.

Your job is what you are paid to do while your work is what you are born to do. A job refers to the specific skills and tasks we perform for a living, while work encompasses our God-given gifts and purpose. Ideally, our jobs and work should overlap, allowing us to engage in labor that fulfills our practical needs and divine calling. This is where we can redefine our work and move from job to vocation.

We can be trained to do a job and acquire skills to earn a paycheck, but it may not be what God has gifted us to do. Transitioning from a job to God-ordained work requires faith and discernment. It's crucial to seek God's guidance on this journey, recognizing that immediate changes may not always be feasible. Once we find out where our gifting is, we might find work that glorifies God and aligns with what we're passionate about.

We miss the abundance of God's blessings because we have tunnel vision about work in a post-Fall world. Some of us get a job merely as a means of self-preservation. I said this earlier, but it bears repeating. Jesus taught His disciples to seek their kingdom assignment (purposeful work) over a job that merely satisfies their basic need for shelter, food, drink, and clothing,

> Therefore, I tell you, stop being worried or anxious (perpetually uneasy, distracted) about your life, as to what you will eat or what you will drink; nor about your body, as to what you will wear. Is life not more than food, and the body more than clothing? Therefore, do not worry or be anxious, saying, "What are we going to eat?" or "What are we going to drink?" or "What are we going to wear?"

> For the pagans and Gentiles eagerly seek all
> these things; but do not worry [about these
> things] for your heavenly Father knows that
> you need them. But first and most impor-
> tantly seek (aim at, strive after) His king-
> dom and His righteousness [His way of
> doing and being right—the attitude and
> character of God], and all these things will
> be given to you also.[i]

According to Maslow's hierarchy of needs, our physiological needs are biological requirements for human
survival, including food, shelter, and clothing. "If these
needs are not satisfied, the human body cannot function
optimally. . . . Other needs become secondary until these
needs are met."[1] We often find ourselves seeking self-preservation, but the cost of that is often being trapped in jobs
that we hate and burying what God has given us.

We may long to follow God's plan for meaningful
work, but we have prioritized our needs although God has
promised to provide for us. When we accept God's provision, we are freed up to pursue work that will do more
than put food on the table and give us shelter, but work
that will outlive and outlast our presence on this planet.

If we need to transition from a job to God-ordained
work, first we should seek God for direction. Perhaps it's
not expedient for us to quit our jobs immediately in pursuit of the work we should be doing. But if we start now to

seek God for our giftings, He will lead us to the work that will allow us to serve, worship, and glorify God.

Second, we should discover what we're passionate about. Our work could center around those things that motivate and inspire us. Figuring that out might give us clues to what God wants us to do.

Third, we must differentiate between passion and lust. Lust for this thing or that will burn out quickly, but our passions never leave. We must discern between fleeting interests and enduring callings. If we find ourselves jumping from one interest to another and never settling on anything, it might be lust and not passion.

We must take our interests to God so we can figure out if it's lust or passion, but we should not walk in fear. Fear doesn't promote; it paralyzes. Fear will make us slaves to our needs and keep us from God's promises. We must trust that God will provide for us and lead us.

As a former executive with a lucrative career, I left the corporate world to pursue teaching people how to harmonize their work with their life's mission. At first, I didn't exactly take a leap of faith as I left my old job. To secure my family, I made sure that my financials and bank accounts were stable enough to leave the job, thinking that the security and provision of my family were solely left up to me.

After a series of poor investment choices and unfortunate circumstances, most of my savings were wiped out. Now I had to rely and depend on God for our long-term provision. Like Abraham, I had to have faith in God even though I didn't know exactly where God was leading us.

When I took a genuine leap of faith and listened to God's voice, I saw God at work even in our finances. My wife and I were led to purchase property for a business we had just launched. I didn't have a stable job, but we went to the bank anyway to pursue a loan.

The banker didn't ask any questions relating to my employment or my ability to pay back the loan since he knew me from my previous corporate job. Instead, they processed the loan, no questions asked. I bought the property for $1.5 million, and after two years, it increased in value to $3 million and continues to rise. The new business took off, the Lord preserved my family, and He proved Himself faithful even though I failed to trust Him fully in the beginning.

My experience forced me to face a crossroads: fear or faith. At first, I chose fear as I put money aside as a safety net because I was in self-preservation mode. But after losing almost all my safety net, I realized that faith is the evidence of the unseen and that God knows how to reward those who diligently seek His will.

I am reminded of David's exhaustive conclusion: "*I would have despaired* had I not believed that I would see the goodness of the LORD in the land of the living."[j] My experience taught me that God will deliver us from the fear of lack, not being able to take care of our families, and losing everything. Faith and fear can co-exist because it is possible to fear but still choose to trust and have faith in God, but your faith must master your fears. I have learned that the antidote for fear is to trust in God.[k]

God Called Us to Work

In the garden, God could have cultivated the land and made every plant needed for man's survival to grow, but instead, He required man's active participation in the marketplace through work, which was man's worship and service to God. God's original intention was not for man to idly worship Him, but to participate with Him by filling the earth with His glory.

God has called us and given us His mandate to dominate over everything except humans. We can't have dominion unless we involve work. Even in the millennial kingdom of Christ, man will continue to work by worshiping God forever.

As God's image bearers, we pattern ourselves after Him. If we look back to the themes of creation theology, we find that God speaks; we speak. God works; we work. God rests; we rest and will be granted ultimate rest upon His return. This rest is not idleness but a state of being free from the dehumanizing systems of the world. In that rest, we won't have oppressive leaders who will abuse those who work for them. We won't do backbreaking drudgery. We will move on to sweatless victories and rewarding work.

When we are obedient to God and mirror Him in what we do, we have the authority and power to work. How can we represent God if we don't do what He does? How can we mirror God if we aren't obedient to His mandate?

The concept of work, as outlined in Genesis, is profoundly intertwined with our purpose and identity as human beings. From the beginning, God's design for humanity included work as a form of worship and service, emphasizing the nobility and significance of our labor. When we embrace God's mandate for work, we restore its purpose. In essence, God calls us to reevaluate our approach to work, urging us to recognize its intrinsic value as part of God's plan and to embrace our roles as co-creators with Him.

Transitioning from a mere job to God-ordained work requires faith, trust, and a willingness to seek God's direction. It challenges us to overcome fear and trust in God's provision, ultimately finding joy and purpose in the work we are called to do. This trust liberates us from the anxiety of self-preservation and allows us to pursue meaningful work that glorifies God. Of course, our physiological needs must be met for us to function optimally. However, we are assured that God is aware of these needs and will provide, freeing us to focus on our higher purpose.

Viewing work as a divine calling transforms it from drudgery to a meaningful pursuit that serves, worships, and glorifies God. As co-creators with Him, our work becomes an expression of obedience and faith, reflecting His glory on earth. By trusting in God's provision and seeking His guidance, we can face the challenges of the post-Fall world and fulfill our divine assignments with joy and purpose.

As we mirror God in our actions—speaking, working, and resting—we not only fulfill our divine purpose but also experience the abundant blessings that come from aligning our lives with His will. In doing so, we reclaim the true essence of work as a noble, purposeful, and worshipful endeavor, reflecting God's image and participating in His ongoing creation.

Chapter Six

The Restoration of Purposeful Work

The restoration of purposeful work and true fulfillment in our labor comes when it is done for God's glory. This worship transcends mere self-serving pursuits and aligns our work with eternal purposes. When we acknowledge that there is a need for our work to regain its purpose and meaning, through faith, we can begin to discover work that honors God as opposed to jobs that keep us from co-creating with God. The notion of worship and service is at the heart of our work and benefits us and others.

God calls us to a higher understanding of work and worship, urging us to consecrate our efforts to God, trust in His provision, and seek His eternal purposes in all we do. Through this, we can experience true fulfillment and make a lasting impact for God's kingdom. The Bible provides a profound insight into the relationship between man and God, emphasizing the significance of serving and worshiping God rather than oneself or material possessions. We must explore the pitfalls of self-worship and the eternal value of dedicating one's work to God.

Upward Worship

After God expelled Adam from the garden, He told him to till the ground from "which he had been made,"[a] pointing Adam back to his source. The word *till* signifies more than agricultural labor; it represents the intrinsic call to serve a higher purpose. Since *till* means "to serve," who was the man serving after he was expelled from the garden? He wasn't worshiping God anymore; he was worshiping himself, a shift from divine reverence to self-centeredness.

This is why Paul wrote "Yes, they knew God, but they wouldn't worship him as God or even give him thanks. And they began to think up foolish ideas of what God was like. As a result, their minds became dark and confused. Claiming to be wise, they instead became utter fools. They traded the truth about God for a lie. So they worshiped and served the things God created instead of the Creator, who is worthy of eternal praise!"[b] When we glorify ourselves or the material world instead of God, we lose sight of our divine purpose.

True worship is upward, directed toward God alone. It cautions against inward (self-focused) and outward (world-focused) worship. While we can admire those things, only God is worthy of our worship. That's why working only for ourselves is empty and meaningless and distracts from the true object of our worship. In modern times, this manifests as working solely for personal gain, whether it's wealth, status, or power. Work done without divine purpose lacks eternal value and is going in the wrong direction, which leaves us void.

We should always work upward, or as unto the Lord. Anything that's done outside God's will is vain glory. The danger of self-worship and the futility of working solely for personal gain is echoed in the teachings of one of the wisest men who ever lived: King Solomon. "So, I came to hate life because everything done here under the sun is so troubling. Everything is meaningless—like chasing the wind."[c] This passage highlights the existential emptiness that accompanies a life centered on the vanity of self-serving endeavors as opposed to the eternal value of God-ordained work.

In contrast, work done for God's glory carries eternal significance and purpose. King Solomon poignantly reflected on the vanity of work done solely for self-satisfaction. If we're working only to please ourselves, it will be soon forgotten when we die. There's no divine value in it and no eternal purpose to our work, but when it is eternal, it will outlive us and benefit others for a lifetime.

When our work is aligned with God's calling, we experience fulfillment and joy. Solomon reminds us that people should eat, drink, and enjoy the fruits of their labor, for these are gifts from God.[d] We don't have to be trapped in oppressive jobs just to make ends meet. When we do God's ordained work, He allows us to be satisfied in what we do.

The rich young ruler struggled to relinquish his wealth to follow Christ. His inability to trust Jesus and let go of his riches serves as a cautionary tale of misplaced trust and missed divine abundance. The ruler's predicament shows the challenge of prioritizing God over material wealth. "Good Master, what shall I do to inherit eternal life?"[e]

After Jesus listed the commandments, the ruler thought he had done all those things. Then Jesus said, "Sell all that thou hast, and distribute unto the poor, and thou shalt have treasure in heaven: and come, follow me."[f] But the man couldn't accept Jesus' terms for eternal life or His invitation to follow God. He "was very sorrowful: for he was very rich."[g]

The ruler's inability to relinquish his riches for the sake of following Jesus serves as a poignant reminder of the spiritual blindness that wealth can cause. Peter then reminded Jesus that he and the other disciples had left everything behind to follow Him. Jesus assured them, "There is no man that hath left house, or parents, or brethren, or wife, or children, for the kingdom of God's sake, Who shall not receive manifold more in this present time, and in the world to come life everlasting."[h]

This is the promise that should reassure us when we're trying to decide between faith and fear. If we're afraid to take that leap of faith, Jesus is telling us that we will be blessed here in this present world as well as in the world to come.

The man's riches blinded him to the abundance he could have had if he had trusted Jesus and given up all to follow Him. Instead of relying on God, he relied on his wealth. But God can do more with what we have than we can. Our hands are too small to control what God has for us, but many of us have a spirit of control and hesitate to surrender fully to God. We believe that if we can't control our destiny, then we don't want to participate. But if we would only give everything over to God, we would see our resources multiply 100 times.

Jesus' parable of the talents illustrates this principle.[i] The man who had five talents and the man who had two talents released what they had and put them to use. In the process, they multiplied the talents 100-fold. But the man who had one talent didn't use it at all. He buried it, and when the master returned, the man still had only one talent.

We may view this as a way to save the talent by not taking the risk of using it and ending up losing it, but the master didn't see it that way. He expected that while he was gone, his servants would be busy working and making a profit on what he had given them. The man with the one talent was wasteful because he earned nothing more than the one talent he was given, and in the end, that one talent was taken away.

This parable emphasizes the necessity of active faith and stewardship, risk and reward, and trusting God to multiply our efforts. Playing it safe is never the answer in God's economy because it comes from a place of fear: *What if I lose what little I have? What if the risk is too great?*

What if I fail? But when we're walking in God's plan for us, we can trust that He will take our little and make much. Solomon reminds us to "commit our works to the LORD [submit and trust them to Him], And our plans will succeed if we respond to His will and guidance."[j]

Believers are called to trust God with their resources, knowing He can multiply their efforts beyond their limited capabilities. We can give everything we have over to Him, and He will meet our needs and more. When we hold so tightly to our resources, we're no different than unbelievers.

But when we worship upward and trust God, we will invoke His divine favor and doors will open for us. Blessings aren't falling out of the sky because they are already all around us and prepared for us. We just need to let God open our eyes to them. When we allow God to focus our minds, we will be able to see far beyond our current circumstances and see things we've never seen before. We will no longer be distracted by drudgery and self-preservation.

We've probably all known people who have had jobs for 40 years, retired, come to the end of their lives, and have nothing eternal to show for all those years. They were never satisfied or at peace. Everything they were striving for was like chasing the wind and profiting them nothing of value.

Set Aside for God's Use: True Holiness

Paul wrote, "I urge you by the mercies of God, to present your bodies [dedicating all of yourselves, set apart] as a living sacrifice, holy and well-pleasing to God, *which is* your rational, logical, intelligent act of worship."[k] The King James Version refers to "act of worship" as "reasonable service."

When we work, it is our bodies that carry out these acts of service or worship. God gave us these bodies, and He wants us to offer ourselves physically to our work and not offer our bodies to other pursuits. Anything offered to God must be consecrated, set apart, for God's use. That's our high worship, our true service.

It's through our sacrifice of ourselves to God that we begin to realize why He created us. He put us on earth with a physical body to till the ground and to co-create with Him. How do we consecrate these bodies to the work of the Lord? We must commit our bodies to be temples of the Holy Ghost. Our bodies must be reserved for God. This role involves not only personal devotion but also active service and witness in the marketplace.

The Old Testament goes into great detail about the items placed inside the tabernacle and the temple. All the items were consecrated and set apart for God's use only. They were not for personal use. If they were used for anything outside their intended purpose, they became defiled, unholy, and no longer acceptable until they were consecrated or set aside again for God's purpose.

God also gives ecclesiastical gifts to the body of Christ to be used exclusively for the edification of the church and advancing His kingdom: the five-fold ministry, God "gave some, apostles; and some, prophets; and some, evangelists; and some, pastors and teachers; For the perfecting of the saints, for the work of the ministry, for the edifying of the body of Christ."[1] When done to glorify God, these gifts are works of service and worship.

Equip means "to make more able," so the purpose of the five-fold ministry is to make the body of Christ more able, to empower us to be more active, effective, and resourceful in accomplishing God's work in the marketplace. *Perfecting (katartismos)* means "equipping; complete furnishing." *Work (ergon)* means "business, employment; anything accomplished by hand; an act, deed, thing done." *Edify (oikodome)* means "to build up; strengthening; to make more able."

The gifts in the church should prepare us for work, service, worship, and domination of the marketplace. When people leave our church services, they should feel they can conquer the world because when they're doing God's work, they can! They should believe they can walk in excellence and be the image-bearers that God created them to be. We must know when we leave our church sanctuaries that we are God's representatives, His vice-regents on the planet.

When God created man, He breathed in man the breath of life, God's Spirit. That's the only thing that gives life. God's Spirit, breathed into us at creation and renewed through the Holy Spirit, empowers us to perform great works for the kingdom.

Life and power are in the Spirit. Just as Jesus told His disciples before His ascension, "But ye shall receive power, after that the Holy Ghost is come upon you: and ye shall be witnesses unto me both in Jerusalem, and in all Judaea, and in Samaria, and unto the uttermost part of the earth."[m] If we want the power to win the world for Christ, we need the Holy Spirit's guidance.

With the Holy Spirit, we can show up as our authentic selves in the marketplace, and no one can do what we do. God has created each of us to be unique, so when we go out to represent God, we don't have to compete or worry about someone else taking our assignment. God has called us to do something uncommon in the earth. We don't have to worry about numbers.

Whether God gives us a storefront or a megachurch, we must work on developing and equipping people instead of building a brand. We should give people the tools to live out their destinies so they don't operate out of fear. Millions of people need what God called us to do. If we stay focused on God's work, the people who need our giftings will come.

Through the presence of the Holy Spirit, the church's dominion power has been restored through Christ. Paul prayed that the believers' eyes would be enlightened to know the incomparably great power available to them, the same power that raised Jesus from the dead and put Him above everything, above all rule and authority, power, and dominion. God has placed all things under His feet, the church being His body.[n]

When my wife and I discussed our work and purpose, we were determined to develop and equip people for marketplace ministry. We walk out our purpose every day whether we are executives, entrepreneurs, or pastors. We sought God's guidance for our purpose and the "why" of our work. We weren't interested in making people emotional in the services. We believed that by equipping and empowering them, they could fulfill their purposes.

We witnessed the impact of our efforts as people shared God's Word and applied it to their lives, creating a ripple effect that drew more people to hear the gospel. We weren't giving them theories that weren't applicable to their lives. We were giving them the tools they needed to work, worship, and serve as unto the Lord.

Three Mighty Men of God

As a senior executive, I gave my employees a mantra to remember if they were seeking promotion at work: PIE (performance, image, and exposure). These are three proven, biblically based principles that apply to any work detail my employees might have encountered. PIE highlights the importance of excellence, integrity, and visibility in our endeavors. God expects us to perform, bear His image, and be exposed to the world. By living out our faith, we attract opportunities to showcase God's work in us.

When Jesus told the parable of the talent, He said that the master's response to the profitable servants was, "Well done, thou good and faithful servant: thou hast been faithful over a few things, I will make thee ruler over many things: enter thou into the joy of thy lord."[b] The master wanted his servants to perform, do excellent work, while he was gone. When he approached the servant who hid his talent and did nothing with it, he did not praise him because the servant had not performed or been profitable.

Our assignment is to bear God's image to the world, not our own.[p] God's not interested in us building our brand or marketing ourselves so we can build a following. If it's not about mirroring God to other people, then our motives are selfish and meaningless.

We must have exposure. What good is it to bear God's image if we can't put that image before other people? "A man's gift maketh room for him, and bringeth him before great men."[q] God will open doors for us to be seen by many people.

Joseph, Daniel, and David exemplify the PIE principle. Despite hardships, they kept working and putting God first. Through slavery, imprisonment, false accusations, adversity, and other struggles, these men continued to serve God.

Joseph went from slave to ruler, and his faithfulness led to his rise in Egypt. He was favored by his father but despised by his brothers. This predicament led to his enslavement and then a false accusation of sexual harassment by Potiphar's wife led to imprisonment, yet he still excelled because God was with him.

In prison, Joseph interpreted dreams for his cellmates but was soon forgotten by those who promised to remember him. Eventually, someone did remember him, which led to his exposure to the king of Egypt, who was troubled by his dreams. Joseph interpreted the king's dream, which eventually led to his promotion to the second-highest position in Egypt.[r]

Daniel's devotion in prayer and leadership brought him favor with the king and eventually transformed the Babylonian Empire toward God. It was said of Daniel's performance that he "proved himself more capable than all the other administrators and high officers. Because of Daniel's great ability, the king made plans to place him over the entire empire."[s]

Daniel was a man of prayer. Even when he was forbidden to pray to God, he prayed anyway, which landed him in the lion's den. God's deliverance of Daniel proved to the king that Daniel's God was superior to all other gods. King Darius then issued "a decree that in every dominion of his kingdom *men must* tremble and fear before the God of Daniel. For He *is* the living God, and steadfast forever; His kingdom *is the one* which shall not be destroyed, And His dominion *shall endure* to the end."[t]

The Spirit of God was with Daniel and, as an image-bearer, he had an excellent spirit, knowledge, and wisdom. He knew how to solve problems in his marketplace, and his work was in service to God, which changed an entire empire.

When God told Samuel to anoint a new king, David wasn't his first choice. Samuel looked at David's seven brothers and wanted to choose one of them because he was tall, strong, and handsome. But God said to Samuel, "Do not look at his appearance or at the height of his stature, because I have rejected him. For the LORD sees not as man sees; for man looks at the outward appearance, but the LORD looks at the heart."[u] Samuel was sure that God had sent him to Jesse's house to anoint the next king of Israel, so he enquired if Jessie had more sons.

Jesse, David's father, then called David in from the sheep fields. When David arrived, the Lord told Samuel, "Arise, anoint him: for this is he."[v] Although Samuel initially doubted David was the king God wanted, David would later perform in such a way that it left no doubt in anyone's mind that he was the rightfully anointed king. He defeated the giant Goliath, and he proved to be a great warrior. He allowed the image of God to shine through his character as he was said to be a man after God's own heart, who was brave and bold.[w] David, the shepherd king, demonstrated his work through acts of bravery and leadership.

Joseph's excellence in adversity led to his elevation in Egypt. Daniel's unwavering faith brought him favor even in a foreign land. David, chosen for his heart rather than his stature, demonstrated remarkable performance and leadership. These men illustrate how performance, image, and exposure, when aligned with God's will, lead to divine promotion and influence.

Their stories of faithfulness, perseverance, and divine favor inspire us to live out our God-given purposes boldly. When we live the PIE mantra, we can turn the world's systems upside down. We can be effective change agents for Christ. The marketplace will never be the same, and companies will say only Christians need apply. That's a powerful witness!

Our unique contributions, empowered by God, can transform the marketplace and draw others to Him. By focusing on God's work, we become powerful witnesses, fulfilling our divine purposes and impacting the world for His glory. As it relates to work, worship and service in Christian theology are intrinsically linked to one's relationship with God. True worship is directed upward toward God, and service is carried out as an expression of that worship.

The pitfalls of self-worship and materialism are contrasted with the eternal value of dedicating one's work to God. By embracing the principles of faithfulness, productivity, and reliance on the Holy Spirit, believers can fulfill their God-given purposes and leave a lasting impact on the world.

The essence of our labor and purpose on earth is intricately linked to our devotion and worship. The distinction between working for ourselves and working for God's glory is fundamental. Serving ourselves leads to vanity and futility while serving God imbues our work with eternal significance and divine value. When we align our efforts with God's will, our labor transcends mere earthly accomplishments and contributes to God's greater plan.

Developing and equipping others is the true measure of success. As my wife and I discovered, our purpose was to empower people to fulfill their divine callings. This approach creates a ripple effect, spreading God's Word and influence far beyond our immediate reach. Our greatest achievements lie in the success of those we equip to serve God in their unique capacities.

By embodying PIE attributes, we not only reflect God's image but also create opportunities for His glory to be revealed through us. Performance reflects our diligence and productivity in God's work. Image denotes our role as bearers of God's image and likeness.

Exposure ensures that our witness reaches others, as King Solomon explains, "A man's gift makes room for him, and brings him before great men."[x] As we navigate our roles in the marketplace, let us remain focused on equipping and empowering others and fostering environments where faith and purpose thrive.

This breath of life is renewed in us through the Holy Spirit, which empowers us for great works. With the Holy Spirit, we can authentically represent God in our workplaces, fulfilling our unique callings without fear of competition. Each believer's contribution is irreplaceable and divinely appointed.

Our work ethic, integrity, and faith can transform workplaces, making them environments where God's principles are honored. This powerful witness showcases the tangible benefits of a life dedicated to God's service. The divine mandate for work extends far beyond mere labor; it is a call to serve God through our daily efforts. By worshiping upward and aligning our work with God's purpose, we infuse it with eternal significance.

Chapter Seven

The Power to Get Wealth

The marketplace is often viewed as a secular domain, distinct from the spiritual realm. However, when we understand our role as co-creators with God, everything we do outside the church also has eternal and lasting implications when we align ourselves with our God-given purpose.

Our activities in the marketplace are not just commercial endeavors but opportunities to further extend God's kingdom on earth as it is in heaven. Furthermore, whatever God has purposed us to do on the earth, He is more than able to provide the necessary resources to accomplish His will and purpose.

The Jewish people had spent 430 years enslaved in Egypt and, at the Exodus, about 600,000 men (not including women and children) were released from Egypt.[a] As they were about to enter into the land God promised them, Moses urged them to remember the Lord their God because it was He who gave them the "ability [power] to produce wealth."[b]

God needed them to understand that nothing they would ever produce was independent of God and that God had divinely empowered them to make a living and create wealth. As we navigate the marketplace, we should expect increase from our work to be realized in spiritual and material gain.

This power is not limited to financial prosperity but extends to the ability to become more efficient, effective, and productive in what we do every day by solving problems, innovating, and improving the world around us. As co-creators, we are called to use this power responsibly and with purpose, always acknowledging that it originates from God.

Many people miss out on living powerful lives due to fear, insecurity, or inaction. This reluctance to embrace divine opportunities and the unwillingness to effectuate change in our environment is a condition of the Fall, which introduced scarcity, poverty, and the fear of both. However, when we align ourselves with God's will and purpose and solely depend on God, He gives us the ability to overcome these limitations and step into a life of abundance and prosperity.

In the marketplace, ministry often takes the form of solving problems. Jesus' parables frequently highlight the importance of stewardship, using our talents to improve life's conditions, and producing tangible benefits.

True wealth in God's economy is not merely about accumulating money for ourselves but encompasses all that we need to meet the needs of others. Paul reminded the church at Corinth that God can make every favor and earthly blessing come in abundance to them so that they may always, under all circumstances, have complete sufficiency in everything and have an abundance for every good work and act of charity.[c] This wealth enables us to share with others and contribute to the common good. We should be proponents of a balanced understanding of wealth as a tool for fulfilling God's purposes.

We Are Problem-Solvers

In 2023, Kimberlyn and I were awakened with an idea that we knew could potentially solve a marketplace challenge that has plagued the education delivery in the school system for as long as I can remember. We were always besieged with complaints of inconsistency, lack of standardization, and the lack of connectivity with the different types of learners in the classroom. So when we were awakened at 3 AM, we got out of bed and wrote down the idea as quickly as it came to us. We got online to see if the idea existed or if some version had already been implemented and discovered that it had not.

We quickly assembled a team of carefully selected people to engage in building out an online portal that would help our instructors deliver consistent, standardized education that connects with all learning types on campus or virtually. The system would also allow students to engage in learning after the classroom lectures to build confidence in the material previously learned. In developing this program, we explored ways to provide more flexibility to staff members and students while reducing facility space and other overhead costs, thereby reducing the overall cost of education.

Because of the idea God gave us early one morning, we now have an exciting education delivery system that is up and running delivering tremendous cost savings across several campuses. Within one year of its launch, we expect this system to be implemented across the country at many different schools producing similar results.

This is just one example of how God gives us the power to get wealth. He engages us to be beneficial in the areas of the marketplace where we are assigned to make things better for our companies, customers, employees, and others who may be affected by our work. We may not be the smartest or most educated in those spaces, but we can be the most faithful at what we do.

The apostle James reminds us that if we lack wisdom, we can ask God, "who gives wisdom to everyone generously without rebuke *or* blame, and it will be given to [us]."[d] It is easy for us to say, "This is not my problem," but what if God has called you into that space for that problem? Will you ignore it and leave it for the next generation, or will you engage in beneficial service beyond your natural ability with the help of God? Could it be that God is nudging you and waiting for you to ask for wisdom?

If my wife and I had gone back to sleep and hadn't nurtured the idea God gave us in the wee hours of the morning, we wouldn't have been involved in this amazing achievement, and we would have missed God's purposeful assignment. Instead, we seized the opportunity as soon as God spoke to us. We didn't hesitate. We immediately said, "What do we need? Where do we get the resources? Let's write this down. Who can we bring together to make this happen? Now let's execute this. Let's find the resources and make a difference in people's lives!"

Since we are co-creators with God, He empowers us to solve problems, improve situations, and make things better. This becomes how we are empowered to get wealth. But even as we improve upon and expand what God has given us, we must never get hung up on this power. We should always remember that it comes from God. He is the one who gives us the creative instincts to innovate and move thoughts from ideation to realization.

Hardwired for Safety

God has given us the power, ability, and might to get wealth, and it is available without discrimination. So why are we not inclined to change our environment? Why are we not making a difference in the marketplace? When God speaks, why are we paralyzed with fear and reluctant to seize opportunities God provides to improve our marketplace conditions?

One explanation is that we are hardwired for safety. We want to improve, and we long for change, but our limbic and reptilian brain, based on the amygdala gland, is always scanning for perceived threats to our physical safety, sense of belonging, and emotional integrity. This gland registers any attempt to change what goes against our "normal."

We are hardwired against a "new normal," so we resist change and try to stick with the status quo. If we feel threatened, the amygdala will secrete hormones that put us in fight or flight mode. It's this reaction that keeps us ensconced in our comfort zones afraid to venture outside.

So when God is pushing us in new directions, our brains perceive that change as a threat and shut us down. But God did not give us the "spirit of fear and timidity"; He has given us the power to overcome, the love to endure, and the self-discipline to achieve beyond our wildest imagination.[e] Although biologically, we're hardwired for self-preservation, which is ideal in certain situations, we must transcend that and trust God with our new normal, whatever that may be.

When we're afraid, we can overcome our fear by trusting the power God has given us to succeed. Fear will tell us all the reasons we can't do something, but God's power gives us the strength to muscle through the noise. It is often what we say with our mouths during moments of fear that determines the outcome.

What we say will sustain or destroy us, so we must be careful what we say because it reflects what we believe.

What we declare with our mouths is what we bring into our reality. Out of the abundance of the heart the mouth speaks,[f] so we should choose our words wisely when we feel fearful or anxious.

Often, when I feel apprehensive and stressed, I reflect on the promises God has given us through the Scriptures. "Now to Him who is able to . . . do superabundantly more than all that we dare ask or think [infinitely beyond our greatest prayers, hopes, or dreams], according to His power that is at work within us."[g] This verse reminds me that I can do infinitely more than I can fathom in my mind or express with my lips. There is nothing beyond my reach or my capabilities, and whatever I need to accomplish my goals, "with all his abundant wealth through Christ Jesus, my God will supply all [my] needs."[h]

The Anatomy of a Problem

People often ask me how they can increase their wealth. I ask them, "What problems are you solving, and how will that be beneficial to other people?" The first rule of business is to find a need and fill it. To be successful is not just about making money, it is about finding ways to improve the lives of others. If we can solve problems—whether for companies, individuals, churches, or consumers—we'll make money. When God completed creation, He said it was very good or beneficial, meaning that everything was created in service of each other.

Before we can solve problems, we must first identify why it is important, which establishes the purpose of the problem. Then we should ask ourselves, *Who will benefit from the resolution of the problem?* This question speaks to the scale of the problem. *What is the end goal? What conditions will be improved as a result of solving this problem?* Then we can consider the methods we will use to solve the problem and how to sustain the change long-term.

As co-creators with God, our assignment is to improve the conditions around us through innovation and creative ideas. When God placed man in the garden to dress and cultivate it, He intended for man to make the garden better, to expand it, and to eliminate the problem of the lack of cultivated plants.[i] Adam was simply harmonizing with God's purposeful design to bring glory to God and fulfill His mandate.

Harmony and synchronicity with creativity allowed man ultimately to produce a chair from the tree that God created and a 747 airplane from the elements that God placed in the ground. God has given us the power to see beyond our current situations and frustrations and see the incredible possibilities that lie ahead of us if we only believe. But that can only happen when we are in sync with God's original will and purpose for creation, and this is how wealth is created in the world and in our lives.

Our ideas don't have to be unique. But if those ideas can solve problems and meet a valuable need in any community, they'll ultimately produce wealth if we stay with them. We're currently mentoring Mignon François, a celebrity baker, who owns an incredibly successful cupcake business. In her book *Made From Scratch*, she says God told her to take the five dollars she had and buy ingredients to make cupcakes to sell to her neighbors.

Mignon went from having five dollars to feed her family to running a multimillion-dollar cupcake empire simply by producing something that met a need. The cupcakes she produces are phenomenal, but the only people who knew this lived in her local community and the surrounding areas. Now she is on a quest to make those delicious cupcakes available around the globe.

When we help people maximize their power to get wealth, it's not about money; it's about solving problems, meeting needs, and serving others. When we developed our education platform, we wanted to improve student outcomes and reduce the cost of education. The impact of that will multiply and touch millions of people we'll never meet. For people passionate about solving problems, the money and resources will eventually come.

In the meantime, as Jesus advised, we shouldn't worry about meeting our basic needs or become stuck in self-preservation mode. The rich young ruler couldn't follow Jesus because he couldn't loosen his grip on his wealth and move past the post-Fall scarcity mindset. Jesus was trying to get him to do something even more profound with his life, and if he had come alongside Jesus and followed him, he would have been able to produce 100 times more than he had.

Soul Wealth vs. Material Wealth

When we talk about wealth, that can look different for different people. When we mention wealth, most people think about money. However, that's from a narrow perspective. In God's economy, wealth can mean anything God has given us internally and externally. When God gives us what we need and more, that's wealth. To have more than we need with enough to spare so we can share with others is wealth.

To be clear, we're not preaching a prosperity gospel. We don't need an extrabiblical "gospel" to understand what God means by prosperity. He wants us to succeed and thrive in every area of our lives. As co-creators with God, we are supposed to be harmonious and in alignment with God's purpose for our lives. When we are, everything else flows from that. When we seek God's kingdom before we seek money, power, position, or other material things, we don't have to worry about self-preservation and our needs because God promises to supply all our needs when we prioritize God and His work for us in the world.[j]

John wrote, "Dear friend, I pray that you may enjoy good health and that all may go well with you, even as your soul is getting along well."[k] This verse confirms that

God cares first and foremost about our souls. After that, everything else will flow to us, including wealth, health, and family, among other things. If our souls are doing well, we don't have to worry about prosperity; it is already available to us. But if we neglect the health of our souls, then we're not aligned with God.

Don't be confused by the world's prosperity. That wealth is temporary, empty, and not eternal. "For what shall it profit a man, if he shall gain the whole world, and lose his own soul?"[1] But according to John, when our prosperity is proportionately connected with our souls, then we have wealth that is eternal. Therefore, this wealth can't just be money; it must transcend it. If our souls aren't prosperous, it doesn't matter how much money we have, we're going to lose everything in the end.

When we're generous and don't hoard because of fear that we'll not have enough, we're wealthy. When we can give without worrying if we'll have enough for ourselves, "a good measure—pressed down, shaken together, and running over will be poured back into you with no space left for more. For the standard of measurement you use when you do good to others, it will be measured to you in return."[m] We can't afford to be stingy or wasteful with God's resources because we don't own anything. It all belongs to God; we're just stewards of those resources. "We brought nothing with us when we came into the world, and we can't take anything with us when we leave it."[n] All we are and all we have belongs to God.

Over the years, Kim and I have learned how to give out of the resources God has given us. We've given generously to our church, mission work, and other causes to help people. At one point, we gave so much money that our accountant said he was worried about our financial future if we continued to give so much. He suggested that we invest more of our money so we could prepare for retirement. Since we do invest, we value the need for prudent investments and the advice of specialized wealth managers. However, we know we can't be of service to others by hoarding our financial resources.

Two Scripture passages inform our investment strategy: "Do not store up for yourselves treasures on earth, where moths and vermin destroy, and where thieves break in and steal. But store up for yourselves treasures in heaven, where moths and vermin do not destroy, and where thieves do not break in and steal."[o] and "If anyone has material possessions and sees a brother or sister in need but has no pity on them, how can the love of God be in that person?"[p] When we talk about getting wealth and sharing, We need to practice what we preach.

Some years ago, we were ministering at a church out of state, and we noticed the church's roof was leaking, so we asked how much it would cost to fix it. They had already gotten an estimate of $30,000 for repairs. We decided, with the help of some of the congregation, to donate the money needed to get the roof repaired. We could have ministered that Sunday morning, ignored what we saw, and gone home. But we saw a need, and because we are God's representatives, we did what needed to be done.

We're not good stewards of God's abundance and power if we see a need and are not moved with the compassion needed to do something about it. As the body of Christ, we must represent God and face out to the world in the best way possible. I am sure the pastor and the congregation would rather not have water seeping through the roof, so that situation presented an opportunity for us to use our resources to solve the problem.

I'm not sharing this story to brag about how much we give to help other people. I'm sharing it to emphasize just how much I believe that God's people should be problem-solvers. I realize everyone can't write a check big enough to pay for other people's roof repairs. But what small problems can we solve? Can we give someone a ride to work? Can we pay for someone else's groceries? To be a problem-solver, perhaps we need to start with what we have and then watch God increase our ability to do more.

As vice-regents with God, helping that church with their roof was solving a problem and helping those church members mirror God's image and likeness to their community. God's ordained purpose for prosperity is to bless other people, and we've found that to be true. That's one of the takeaways we can glean from Jesus' parables on the talents. The master gave one servant five talents, another servant two talents, and the other servant one talent. When he returned from his journey, there was a reckoning or accounting of what the servants had done with his money while he was gone. It wasn't their money, but he had given them the latitude to improve and increase the money just as God does with us.

We should have the same perspective on wealth that God does. In the garden of Eden, the riverbeds contained gold.q Adam didn't hurry to dig up all the gold he could find and hoard it or hide it. In the garden, there was no scarcity. God provided everything in abundance. The reason we are tempted to hoard money and worry about every penny is that in our post-Eden world, we have a scarcity mindset. Along with scarcity comes poverty, sickness, and death. That's not God's original intent for us. That's why Jesus said, "Take no thought, saying, What shall we eat? or, What shall we drink? or, Wherewithal shall we be clothed? . . . But seek ye first the kingdom of God, and his righteousness; and all these things shall be added unto you."r

Jesus wants to shift our attention from temporal concerns to what He set in motion at creation: (1) He called us good (beneficial). (2) He made us co-creators and vice-regents with Him. (3) He provided what we need so we are freed to participate in purposeful work. (4) He provided man with the power to get wealth.

We get trapped by the ephemeral attitude of time, space, and matter; but God sees us in eternity. There's no scarcity in Him. He already knows our future, and He has provided for us to get wealth. We may not see it immediately, but we don't have to. God invites us to come alongside Him and not worry about the things He has already solved.

Money Myths

There is purpose in everything that God creates, even prosperity. There are no accidents or coincidences in creation, so everything God created has a design and purpose ordained for its use. In early creation, the river Pishon that wound through the entire land of Havilah had gold in it. Aromatic resin and onyx, considered of great value, were also present in the garden of Eden.[5] All of these precious materials were created by God for a purpose.

"When we don't understand God's purpose for a thing, abuse is inevitable."[1] The word *abuse* means "abnormal use." When we use something abnormally, we destroy or pervert the purpose for which the thing is created. God created gold, the basis for the money we use to transact commerce. We need to know the purpose of money, wealth, and prosperity, or we risk abusing what God intended us to enjoy. When we don't understand the purpose of money, we might embrace common myths about it. Here are four myths that believers need to dispel:

God wants us to be poor. Some Christians believe that being poor is synonymous with holiness. They think the poorer we are, the closer we are to God. Paul wrote concerning Jesus, "Though he was rich, yet for your sakes he became poor, that ye through his poverty might be rich."[t] If God wanted us to be poor, He wouldn't have sent His Son so we could be rich.

The question we should ask about Paul's statement is, "At what point was Jesus rich"? We know that God created everything and that everything belongs to Him. "Without Him nothing was made that has been made."[u] Before he came to earth, Jesus had all the possessions of His Father, which made Him infinitely rich. Then when He became flesh, He divested Himself of His royal regalia so that He could "empathize with all of our weaknesses and infirmities and be tempted in every way, just as we are."[v]

Jesus became poor and was subject to poverty, the same condition we face. The word *poor* in this context means more than "lacking money." Poverty is part of our infirmities. After the Fall, we are spiritually, physically, and emotionally poor without God. But we became rich when we became joint heirs with Christ[w] to share in the godly inheritance of God the Father.

We often hear that money is the root of all evil, but that's a misquotation of the Scripture. Paul said, "The *love* of money is the root of all evil."[x] (emphasis added). Money is not the root of evil; it's an inanimate object and therefore morally neutral. It's the love of money, the obsession with hoarding money, and greed that are evil. If God thought money was evil, He wouldn't have placed gold in the riverbed of the Pison River and other precious stones in the garden of Eden. It's when we fall in love with money and not its Creator that we are in trouble with God.

It's hard for a rich person to go to heaven. This is a misunderstanding of Scripture. Many people read about the rich young ruler in Mark's Gospel and assume it's hard or impossible for rich people to go to heaven. But upon closer observation, we find that this is what Jesus said.

> And Jesus looked round about, and saith unto his disciples, How hardly shall they that have riches enter into the kingdom of God! And the disciples were astonished at his words. But Jesus answereth again, and saith unto them, Children, how hard is it for them *that trust in riches* to enter into the kingdom of God! It is easier for a camel to go through the eye of a needle, than for a rich man to enter into the kingdom of God. And they were astonished out of measure, saying among themselves, Who then can be saved? (emphasis added)[y]

Just as we established that it's the love of money that's evil and not money itself, Jesus tells us that the problem is not with those who are rich but with those who have great affection for money. If they're rich and greedy or love their wealth more than they love God, that's what keeps them out of heaven. "Have I put my trust in money or felt secure because of my gold? Have I gloated about my wealth and all that I own? . . . If so, I should be punished by the judges, for it would mean I had denied the God of heaven."[z]

And what defines what is rich? What's the dollar amount that determines if we're rich? We may be surprised how God defines what it means to be rich. If we have enough and to spare, are we rich? But if we refuse to share what we have, wouldn't that put us in the same category as a rich person who won't share? The ruler chose his wealth over the Source of his wealth, and that could apply to us, too. How many times do we worship the creature more than the Creator? How many times do we put our possessions before God?

You can't serve God and have money. Jesus taught, "No one can serve two masters. Either you will hate the one and love the other, or you will be devoted to the one and despise the other. You cannot serve both God and money."[aa] We can't serve God and money or anything else, but we can certainly serve God and have money. The rich young ruler missed out on following Jesus and the privilege of heaven because he served his wealth more than the One who gave it to Him.

When Jesus was in the wilderness fasting for 40 days, the devil tried to tempt Him from following God's purpose for his life. Before the devil left Jesus, he showed Jesus all the riches of the world and said, "All this I will give you, if you will bow down and worship me." Jesus said to him, "Away from me, Satan! For it is written: 'Worship the Lord your God, and serve him only.'"[bb] When we serve God in His rightful place, the power to get wealth will come and all that comes with it. When we put God first, we invoke the kingdom principle that causes our gifts to return to us in full and running over in our laps.[cc]

Jesus was poor. Paul emphasized in his writings that though Jesus was rich, "yet for [our] sakes he became poor."[dd] This dispels the myth that Jesus was inherently poor. He was incalculably rich before He came to earth. He became (an act of his sovereign will) poor and took on the frailty of the human condition so He could be touched by our spiritual, financial, physical, and emotional poverty. Jesus is always willing to meet us where we are, but He doesn't intend for us to stay there. His intention is to bring us up to Him. Though He "became poor," it was so that we might become rich and participate in His royal inheritance as joint heirs.

The Purpose of Wealth

Understanding the purpose of wealth and money helps us to use money for the reason it was intended in the first place. God's purpose for prosperity is multifaceted and designed to provide for what we need but also deliver us from the entrapment of the world.

First, God intends to free us from the dependency on the world's system of wealth and an insatiable appetite for more. We are warned to watch out and be on guard against all kinds of greed because life does not consist of an abundance of possessions.[ee] The world system is to chase after money by all means necessary, but we are not defined by our cars, houses, or bank accounts. We will ultimately be defined by the fulfillment of our purpose.

Second, God gives us the power to get wealth to ensure that we have all we need and then some. "And God is able to make all grace [every favor and earthly blessing] come in abundance to you, so that you may always [under all circumstances, regardless of the need] have complete sufficiency in everything [being completely self-sufficient in Him], and have an abundance for every good work and act of charity."[ff] Biblical prosperity is like having a prepaid American Express Black Card, you have it when you need it. God provides all we need so we don't have to worry or live in survival mode.

Third, biblical prosperity enables us to do the good work that God has purposed for us to do at the time we are called on to do it. Paul reminds us that "we are His workmanship [His own master work, a work of art], created in Christ Jesus [reborn from above—spiritually transformed, renewed, ready to be used] for good works, which God prepared [for us] beforehand [taking paths which He set], so that we would walk in them [living the good life which He prearranged and made ready for us]."[gg]

Everything we need to help us do what God has called us to do has already been prepared and prearranged on the path God has called us to take. God is not despotic and will never call for what He has not already provided for. He will never demand of us anything that He has not already equipped and enabled us to do.

Understanding our role as co-creators with God transforms our approach to the marketplace. It elevates our work from mere economic activity to a form of ministry that extends God's kingdom on earth. By embracing divine inspiration, responsibly wielding the power to create wealth, and practicing generosity, we fulfill our mandate to steward God's resources and bless others.

As we learn more about how to minister in the marketplace with this perspective, we become conduits of God's grace and provision, demonstrating that true prosperity encompasses material and spiritual abundance. This alignment with God's original design brings fulfillment, purpose, and eternal rewards.

We are called to use our creativity, skills, and resources to advance His kingdom. This involves creating wealth, not for selfish gain, but as a tool for solving problems, improving lives, and serving others. By dispelling myths about wealth and embracing our mandate to steward creation, we can transform the marketplace and bring God's kingdom values into every aspect of our work.

Chapter Eight

The Covenant of Prosperity

"Remember the LORD your God. He is the one who gives you power to be successful, in order to fulfill the covenant He confirmed to your ancestors with an oath."[a] Moses told the children of Israel that they were "empowered to get wealth" to fulfill the covenant God made to their ancestors. The word *covenant* is not a word we customarily use in our society today, but it had significant meaning in the ancient Near East. A *covenant* is "an agreement enacted between two parties where one or more make promises under oath to perform or restrain from certain actions stipulated in advance."[1]

The covenants in the Bible offer profound insights into God's unchanging nature and His redemptive plan for humanity. From the assurance of preservation in the Noahic covenant to the promise of blessings in the Abrahamic covenant, the guidance of the Mosaic covenant, and the ultimate salvation in the New Covenant through Christ, these divine agreements underscore God's commitment and love. Believers are called to embrace these covenants, live by faith, and trust God's promises, fulfilling His original design for a prosperous and blessed life.

Knowing God's excellent track record with covenants stretching back to the Old Testament, we can be confident that God is a God who keeps His Word. God has promised to take care of us, and we can rest in His faithfulness as we continue to work and represent God in the marketplace.

Dispensational Covenants

When we study the covenants, the Bible unveils God's relentless commitment to humanity. These covenants, established by God throughout history, emphasize their enduring significance and the divine promises embedded in them. From the Noahic covenant to the Abrahamic covenant of promise to the Mosaic covenant of conduct, each covenant reveals a facet of God's unchanging purpose and His redemptive plan for mankind.

God's love for humanity reaches its zenith with the Christ covenant, the new covenant of grace, wherein believers are grafted into the promises given to Abraham. This covenant underscores the transition from the law to grace, which offers a profound understanding of God's mercy and the ultimate sacrifice of Jesus Christ.

The covenants reflect God's original design for humanity as laid out in Genesis and the overarching theme of returning to God's initial blueprint. The Old Testament covenants have an enduring relevance considering Christ's fulfillment of the law and the grace available to believers today.

Noahic covenant (the covenant of human preservation[b]): This covenant assured Noah that God will never again destroy the world by flood but will preserve the stability of nature and guarantee that it will function as God originally designed it. As a sign of this covenant, God placed the rainbow in the sky to remind us of His mercy toward us through His promise not to destroy the world again.

Abrahamic covenant (the covenant of promise[c]): In this covenant, God promised Abraham that He would bless him and make his name great. He further promised that his descendants would be great and that the rest of the families on earth would be blessed through him.

Mosaic covenant (the covenant of conduct[d]): This is a covenant between God and the people of Israel that He would be their God and they would be His people, His treasured possession. It has little bearing on us today, but it has preserved the children of Israel to this day, even though they're outside the relationship with God. In the end, they will not see ruin and will be brought back into God's covenant relationship.

Christ covenant (the new covenant of grace[e]): This covenant is a promise from God to forgive sins and restore eternal fellowship with people who turn their hearts toward Him because of Christ's death on the cross. This covenant also confers the blessing of Abraham to all who believe. Paul writes, "And if ye be Christ's, then are ye Abraham's seed, and heirs according to the promise."[f] "The promise" refers to the Abrahamic covenant. So when we receive Christ, God grafts us into the Abrahamic covenant, which promises that God will bless us and cause us to be a blessing to other people as well.

Bless (Hebrew, *barack*) is often used for other definitions, but in this context, it means "to empower." We are empowered (*barack*) to prosper, and if God has empowered us to prosper, nothing can stop the plan of God for our lives.[g]

The Certainty of the Covenant

A covenant oath confirms or seals a legal agreement between two or more parties. Covenants invariably include promises and conditions and are sometimes ratified with blood. The covenant God made to Abraham to bless and protect his descendants was ratified with the blood of animals and birds, but the oath was made to Himself.[h]

> When God made his promise to Abraham, since there was no one greater for him to swear by, he swore by himself, saying, "I will surely bless you and give you many descendants." And so after waiting patiently, Abraham received what was promised. People swear by someone greater than themselves, and the oath confirms what is said and puts an end to all argument. Because God

wanted to make the unchanging nature of his purpose very clear to the heirs of what was promised, he confirmed it with an oath. God did this so that, by two unchangeable things in which it is impossible for God to lie, we who have fled to take hold of the hope set before us may be greatly encouraged.[i]

Regardless of what might be going on in our lives right now, there should be no doubt that God is committed to blessing us. It is the same commitment God made to Adam when God blessed Adam and commanded him to be fruitful and productive. God was so serious about blessing Abraham that He demonstrated His commitment by establishing two immutable things, two unchangeable frameworks through which He guaranteed success. He gave Abraham a promise and sealed it with an oath that can never be broken. When we align ourselves with God's will and purpose for our lives, we are assured of everything we need to complete our mission.

God's covenant oath not only assures us that He will never change His mind, but He will not delay His promise as some people may think of delays. He is timely and purposeful in everything that He does. If there is ever a perceived delay in God's response to us, it is often that He is patiently waiting for us to decide on the path we are going to take. As co-creators, we are called to fulfill our God-ordained kingdom assignment.

God is not obligated to resource every whimsical idea or plan that we have conjured up in our minds, but He doesn't lack any resources for us to fulfill the assignment He has called us to do. His commitment to prosper us is permanent and immutable. He "is effectively at work in you, both to will and to work [that is, strengthening, energizing, and creating in you the longing and the ability to fulfill your purpose] for His good pleasure."[j]

God's immutable promises give us reason to hope. A sure and unbreakable hope that anchors our minds and our emotions and keeps us steady in adverse and challenging situations.[k] We don't have to worry about what we eat, drink, or wear because those basic needs are already guaranteed. We don't have to worry about acceptance or validation because God has created us for this moment. We don't have to worry about our ability or the strength to succeed because He has granted us the power to prosper. God, however, is waiting for us to elevate our minds to the greater things that He has ordained for us to do and to know that He can do infinitely more if we but ask.

A Covenant of Provision

The covenant of prosperity we have with God is His guarantee that He will bless us no matter what happens. We don't have to work for it or earn it. God always honors His promises because He's a God who cannot lie.[l] If God said He will provide our needs, we need no other body of evidence to come in agreement with those words because the faith to believe is predicated on God alone. Through faith, we are convinced of God's promises toward us and can bring them into our imagination even though we may not see physical evidence of what's promised.

However, as co-creators, we are called to act on what we believe and not what we see. When Kim and I got a vision early one morning on how to solve a persistent problem at work, we didn't go back to sleep or delay bringing the right people and resources together. We acted right away because without our actions, or "works," our vision would have been dead on arrival.

Purposeful actions require focus. Actions without focus will have us walking in circles not achieving anything. With over 50,000 thoughts a day swirling through our minds, it's easy to get distracted. But vision is an arrested thought that focuses the mind and allows us to push distractions to the side and see what God is telling us. When we're focused, we will see the opportunities in our path. If we're not focused, we'll miss them.

Through the covenant of prosperity, we can be sure that God will bless and provide for us. We don't have to fear that God will break His promises. However, we may experience delays of the promise, not on God's part, but because we may have taken a detour that God didn't ordain or we were disobedient and needed time for correction. God's timing is always perfect, but He is patient as He waits for us to come into proper alignment with His purpose.

It's also important for us to understand that receiving anything from God is entirely up to us. We can't refuse God's blessings and then complain that He has withheld them from us. Whatever God bestows on us, it's up to us to receive it. If we ignore them or set them aside, there are consequences for our actions.

For example, "For God so loved the world, that he gave his only begotten Son, that whosoever believeth in him should not perish, but have everlasting life."[m] God has kept His part of the bargain. He gave His Son as a gift to us, a gift of salvation, but it's up to us to accept the gift. If we don't, we will experience the consequences of that decision.

God wants us to receive His blessings and share them with others. But as we live in God's blessings, we should be cautious to avoid certain pitfalls and inordinate desires. On one occasion, Jesus cautioned His disciples to watch out and guard against all kinds of greed.[n] This caution is necessary because we possess the propensity for lust and greed.

The "world offers only a craving for physical pleasure, a craving for everything we see, and pride in our achievements and possessions."[o] if you are going to succeed as a marketplace leader, you must first overcome, or at best, fight against these impulses as they cannot be part of your character.

As kingdom leaders and co-creators, we must do the prerequisite work of aligning our character with Christ's. First, we should empty ourselves of ourselves. In other words, we must get rid of our fleshly pride and ambitions that would cause us to be self-centered and worship possessions over purpose. Second, we should immerse ourselves in the Word of God so we can better understand how God wants us to conduct our lives in the world with the proper worldview.

The Bible speaks of operating our lives by the fruit of the Spirit, which tells us to allow the life of Christ to inform our thoughts, decisions, and actions. When we're filled with the Holy Spirit, it's not just a one-off experience. Rather, it's a daily walk with God and always reflecting on how Christ would handle the contemporary decisions of our day.

When we speak of the fruit of the Spirit[p] in our lives, we are talking about the character of love, joy, peace, patience, kindness, goodness, faithfulness, gentleness, and self-control that is present in the life of Christ. These qualities are better than what the culture of our day offers.

For example, the culture tells us we deserve to be happy. But happiness is fleeting and is predictive of our circumstances, whether good or bad. And since we can't control our circumstances, we never know from one day to the next if we will be happy. But God offers us joy, which is an assurance that all things will work out for good as God purposes them. So joy can be present at all times since God will never change His mind about our future. This divine joy serves as an anchor in the stormiest seas and as a rock when everything else feels like sand.

Self-control is another fruit of the spirit that protects us from excesses. Self-control is the ability to resist temptations and impulses as it relates to our thoughts, emotions, or behaviors. It helps us avoid conforming to worldly things and guides our decisions. Self-control is not about how we feel or our personalities but what we choose to do, which is necessary as we gain power, influence, and wealth.

Many people will tell us how we should act or what attitude we should take as we gain wealth, but self-control is derived from the love of God, which informs how we deal with ourselves and other people around us. None of us just wake up the next day and suddenly are perfected in self-control. This will take time, intentional focus, and help from the Holy Spirit. Please know that what we focus on is what we develop, and anything we don't focus on will never grow in our lives.

Living in the Covenant of Prosperity

As marketplace leaders, how do we live in the reality of God's covenant to prosper us? How do we activate the things God has already prepared and made available to us even in the marketplace?

First, remember that God knows the plan for our lives. His plan is to prosper us and give us hope and a future.[q] Since God has the original plan for our lives, we don't have to treat our lives like a do-it-yourself project. We must consult God to see what He sees and knows about us. We can't limit God with our small thinking or timidity. Because we are hardwired for safety, we are prone to dumb things down to where we feel most comfortable. But the greatest that God has planned for us does not reside in our comfort; it resides in our willingness to reach beyond our limitations and tap into what God sees for us.

When His disciples were caught in a storm, Jesus walked on the water to get to them. They were afraid that they might succumb to the tempestuous waves of the sea, but when the disciples saw Jesus, only Peter requested to come to Jesus on the sea. It is better to walk with Jesus on stormy seas than to hang out comfortably in our boats. When imagination is mixed with faith, we will not notice the obstacles in our path, or they will appear less threatening to our future. It is through imagination that innovation and creativity abound. Everything we co-create comes from a thought or an idea that comes from the mind of the Creator. Imagination increases when it is exposed to a problem.

Second, agree with God's priority for our lives. We have many ideas about what our lives should be and what we want to do. But Matthew reminds us to aim for and "be concerned above everything else with the Kingdom of God and with what he requires of [us,] and he will provide [us] with all these other things"[r] that we need.

There is no greater priority than to be what God has created us to be, and this is holiness personified! Everything else would make us behave like fish out of water: floundering, suffocating, and gasping for air. Our power, genius, and influence lie in the will of God. But when we agree with God's priorities, He is responsible for our prosperity needs. "The blessings of the LORD shall come upon you and overtake you, because you obey the voice of the LORD your God."[s]

Third, we must say only what God says about our lives. Solomon cautioned that "death and life is in the power of the tongue and that those who love it and indulge in it will eat its fruit and bear the consequences of their words."[t] So we should speak words of affirmation over our lives, words that can uplift us instead of tearing us down. It is okay not to take ourselves seriously all the time, but we shouldn't make it a habit of speaking self-deprecating words that may undermine who we are. Daily, we should speak words that affirm what God says about us and how

He sees us through the strength of Christ! Here are ten affirmations we should confess over our lives every day.

1. I am strong.
2. I can do all things.
3. I am triumphantly victorious.
4. No weapon formed against me will ever succeed.
5. I am the head and not the tail, above and not beneath, a lender and not a borrower.
6. All things are working out for my good.
7. The joy of the Lord is my strength.
8. I do not have the spirit of fear but of power, love, and sound judgment.
9. All things are possible for me.
10. God shall supply all my needs.

These words of affirmation can transform our lives if we believe them, and we will "bear the consequences" of these words.

Finally, we must live lives driven by faith and not by emotion or our physical senses. Abraham, the father of faith, was given the promise that he would become the father of many nations. However, he was 75 years old and had no children. He didn't see the promise come to pass for 25 years after it was given. By then, he was 100 years old. "Even when there was no reason for hope, Abraham kept hoping—believing that he would some day receive what God had promised."[u] He did not consider his body dead, though he should have, neither the deadness of his wife's womb at 90 years old. He refused to waver at the promise of God but stood strong in faith.

Often, we consider things that are antithetical to the promise of God. But the very consideration of those things weakens our faith. When God makes a promise, we ought to believe it and visualize it as if it is presently there. Faith is the evidence of the unseen, and at the same time, it is the assurance of our hope.

As we navigate the marketplace, we can be assured that God is on our side and that He alone can direct our path. We were made for this moment, and all the resources we need are available to us now to do immeasurably more than we can ask or imagine. We can continue to co-create with God, solve problems, and make the environment better than when we arrived.

We are the salt of the earth, and it is through us that the world is being preserved right now. As we say yes to God's assignment, we will see God do mighty things through us. We might suffer and experience hardship, but I promise you, "the juice is worth the squeeze."

Go change the world!

Notes

Chapter 1

[1]"Church Attendance of Americans 2022," published by Veera Korhonen, Statista (June 2, 2023); Statista.com.

Chapter 2

[1]"7 Reasons Why the Marketplace Is a Great Place for Christians," by Darren Shearer, Theology of Business Institute.

Chapter 3

[1]Based on "Theology of Creation in 12 Points," by Dr. Don A. Carson (desiringgod.org).

[2]*The Wycliffe Bible Encyclopedia* (Moody Pub, 1975).

[3]"Characteristics of God," Dr. Kevin Meador (2005).

Chapter 4

[1]"The Heart of Leadership: Becoming a Servant Leader," by John Maxwell (maxwellleadership.com).

Chapter 5

[1]"You Will Spend 90,000 Hours of Your Lifetime at Work. Are You Happy?" by Kassandra Vaughn, Medium (May 5, 2018).

[2]"Onesimus," *Encyclopedia of the Bible*, Bible Gateway.

[3]"What Is God's Glory," by John Piper, desiringgod.org (July 22, 2014).

[4]"Maslow's Hierarchy of Needs," by Saul McLeod, SimplyPsychology, May 21, 2018 (canadacollege.edu).

Chapter 7

[1]*Understanding the Purpose and Power of Women: God's Design for Female Identity*, by Myles Munroe (Whitaker House, 2018).

Chapter 8

[1]"Covenant," *The Yale Anchor Bible Dictionary*.

Scripture Index

Unless otherwise noted, all Scripture references
are from the Amplified Bible (AMP).

Chapter 1

Chapter 2

Chapter 5

qProverbs 18:16, KJV

rGenesis 29:2-4

sDaniel 6:3, NLT

tDaniel 6:26, NKJV

u1 Samuel 16:7

v1 Samuel 16:12

w1 Samuel 13:14; 17:36

xProverbs 18:16, NKJV

Chapter 7

aExodus 12:37, NIV

bDeuteronomy 8:18, NIV

c2 Corinthians 9:8

dJames 1:5

e2 Timothy 1:7, NLT

fLuke 6:45

gEphesians 3:20

hPhilippians 4:19, GNT

iGenesis 2:5, NET

jMatthew 6:33

k3 John 1:2

lMark 8:36, KJV

mLuke 6:38

n1 Timothy 6:7

oMatthew 6:19-20, NIV

p1 John 3:17, NIV

Chapter 8